DECISIONS,
DECISIONS

DECISIONS, DECISIONS

HOW
(AND HOW NOT)
TO MAKE THEM

DAVE SWAVELY

P U B L I S H I N G

P.O.BOX 817 • PHILLIPSBURG • NEW JERSEY 08865-0817

Unless otherwise indicated, Scripture quotations are from the *NEW AMERICAN STANDARD BIBLE®*. ©Copyright The Lockman Foundation 1960, 1962, 1963, 1968, 1971, 1972 1973, 1975, 1977. Used by permission.

Italics in Scripture quotations indicate emphasis added.

Page design by Tobias Design
Typesetting by Michelle Feaster

Printed in the United States of America

Library of Congress Cataloging-in-Publication Data

Swavely, David, 1966–
    Decisions, decisions : how (and how not) to make them /
Dave Swavely.
        p.   cm.
    Includes bibliographical references.
    ISBN 0-87552-592-X (paper)
    1. Decision making—Religious aspects—Christianity.
2. Decision making—Biblical teaching. I. Title.

BV4509.5 .S93 2002
248.4—dc21
                                                2002033388

CONTENTS

INTRODUCTION

Life is made up of decisions too numerous to count. We each are faced with so many choices every day that people have often been given to say, with anxiety or desperation, "Decisions, decisions!" Every decision leads inevitably to another, and we often have several such series of decisions going on at the same time.

We make choices, and then our choices make us (or break us!). This is true of "big" decisions, of course—the ones we agonize over as we approach them, and often regret horribly after we have made them. But the "little" decisions are just as important, because they lead to the big ones. Consider this example from my life:

About ten years ago, I decided to marry my wife Jill. That was a big decision (though not a difficult one!), but I never would have married her if I had not developed a relationship with her; I never would have developed a relationship with her if I had not seen her love for Christ, while praying with her; I never would have prayed with her if I hadn't decided to meet weekly for prayer with the Senior Class Officers at a Christian high school; I never would have decided to do that if I had not attended their senior class retreat at the beginning of the school year and seen the great need for revival in the school; I never would have attended the retreat if I had not been asked to go by the school's administrator; I never would have been asked to go if I had not gone to lunch one day with that administrator and discussed my possible involvement with the school; and of course I never would have gone to lunch with him if I had not decided to spend my lunch hour that way on that particular day!

So one decision to eat lunch with that man eventually led to marriage with my life partner. And the fact is, every decision you make has that kind of potential ramifications! In that sense, there is no such thing as a "small decision." All of our choices are threads in the fabric of our future. That is why you need to learn how to make good decisions. In fact, you need to learn it so well that you will be able to make the best choice immediately and instinctively, because you often will have little time for extended deliberation.

If you are a believer in Christ, the resulting effects in your life should not be your only motivation, or even your primary one, to make good decisions. The apostle Paul wrote, "We have as our ambition [at all times] . . . to be pleasing to Him" (2 Cor. 5:9) and "Whatever you do, do all to the glory of God" (1 Cor. 10:31). Our heavenly Father will hold us accountable for the choices we make, disciplining us in love when we make wrong ones and blessing us when we follow the principles of his Word. This is the ultimate reason why the way we make decisions is so important: it has ramifications beyond this life and into eternity. Jesus said, "Do not lay up for yourselves treasures upon earth, where moth and rust destroy, and where thieves break in and steal. But lay up for yourselves treasures in heaven, where neither moth nor rust destroys, and where thieves do not break in and steal; for where your treasure is, there will your heart be also" (Matt. 6:19–21).

According to Jesus, your decisions are determined by what is in your heart (cf. Mark 7:21), and their results will also affect what is in your heart (see the last verse above). That is why God is so concerned with your decisions, because he cares so deeply about your heart. Therefore, the way you make decisions is a central part of your personal relationship with God. The importance of this area of your life cannot be overstated, and by God's grace this book will help you to make decisions that honor the Lord and benefit you, as well as help you to avoid some common errors that can rob you of joy and send you spinning in the wrong direction.

Keep in mind as you read the book that, although it focuses primarily on the human responsibility of wise decision making, the concepts of God's leading and guidance are reflected and explained as well. As you learn how to make good decisions, you will be learning how God leads and guides his children according to the Word (and also how he does *not*).

There are several reasons why this book starts with a lengthy discussion of how *not* to make decisions. First, I believe that many Christians already have misconceptions in their minds about how God leads us, and the biblical plan presented later in the book will be easier to understand and accept after those errors have been eliminated. Examining what is wrong first and then presenting the truth is a teaching tool used by Jesus himself in much of his teaching, particularly the Sermon on the Mount ("Do not be like the Pharisees, who . . ."). Also, as you read through the discussion about common misunderstandings, much of the truth about decision making will hopefully begin to take shape in your mind, so that the second half of the book will complete the picture. So don't allow yourself to get too discouraged in the first half! You will be gaining wisdom and discernment that you will need to practice God's way of making good decisions.

PART ONE

HOW *NOT* TO MAKE DECISIONS

ONE ROADS TO NOWHERE

Which ways do you *not* want to go when faced with a life-changing decision (big or small)?

As I mentioned in the introduction, Jesus showed us that we can learn about what is right by first considering what is wrong. But even though our Lord set this example, I am hesitant to take his approach at the beginning of this book, because I fear that it might alienate some readers, who will be tempted to put the book aside before going any further. This may be especially true of many Christians who have a different perspective than I do regarding the cessation of revelation and the "sign gifts." But if you find yourself disagreeing with what I say in the early chapters, I want to encourage you to continue reading anyway, because I believe that the principles in the rest of the book will be helpful to you. I also ask you to read these early sections with an open mind, willing to accept whatever the Lord may say to you through his Word.

If you already know that you will agree with what I say, you may be tempted to skip these chapters, but please don't! What we discuss here will be foundational in many ways to what comes after. And as we will learn, even Christians who are not "charismatic" tend to fall into these same problems, despite their theology.

So let's begin with an imaginary scenario that hopefully will be interesting and helpful in the process of learning about the most common errors in decision making. Suppose your church is sending out a summer missions team to Russia. Before they leave for their trip, the pastor asks them to stand before the congregation in a row, and to briefly explain why they decided to participate in the team, or how God led them to do so. The first four members answer in this way:

1. "I decided to go because I want to have more power in the church and this is one way to get it."
2. "I took a deck of cards and said if I pick anything higher than a ten, I'll go."
3. "An angel appeared to me and told me that I should go."
4. "God gave me a sign. I turned on CBS News and Dan Rather spoke in Russian for a whole hour."

Each of those missions team members had some wrong thinking in their decision-making process. In fact, they illustrate four approaches to decision making that I believe are entirely erroneous ideas. Later we will discuss some misunderstood and misapplied ideas, which contain some truth, but the ones in these first three chapters have nothing whatsoever to commend them. Because these approaches will lead you astray, you should never make decisions based on selfish motives, superficial methods, special revelation outside the Bible, or supernatural signs.

SELFISH OR SINFUL MOTIVES

It should be apparent to Christians that making decisions based on selfish or sinful motives is a wrong approach because that is the way of the world. People everywhere are "looking out for number one." The primary (or only) question on their minds is "What is best for me?" Unfortunately this kind of thinking has infiltrated the church in the form of "needs theology"—the idea that our needs must be met first before we can really reach out to others.[1]

Because of that false teaching and because of the sinful tendencies in all of us, even believers sometimes approach decisions thinking of ourselves first. The biggest issue on our minds is not what God wants or what is best for others, but merely "What can I gain from this?" This is unbiblical thinking, of course. Philippians 2:3–4 says,

> Do nothing from selfishness or empty conceit, but with humility of mind let each of you regard one another as more important than himself; do not

merely look out for your own personal interests, but also for the interests of others.

When the apostle Paul met Jesus Christ in a blinding light on the road to Damascus, Paul's response was "What shall I do, Lord?" (Acts 22:10), and that remains the attitude of all who are walking in the light:

> You were formerly darkness, but now you are light in the Lord; walk as children of light (for the fruit of the light consists in all goodness and righteousness and truth), *trying to learn what is pleasing to the Lord.* (Eph. 5:8–10)

According to the Word of God, when you are primarily concerned with yourself, rather than the glory of God and the good of others, you are on the wrong road and will not make a good decision. When faced with a choice, remember the old saying that the road to JOY is Jesus, Others, then You—in that order.

It should also be obvious that any other motives that are called sinful in Scripture should play no part in your decisions. Watch out for "worldly" motives, as defined by 1 John 2:16: "All that is in the world, the lust of the flesh and the lust of the eyes and the boastful pride of life, is not from the Father, but is from the world." So the mission team member who wanted power in the church was way off, to say the least.

SUPERFICIAL OR WHIMSICAL METHODS

Some people will tell you that the way to make decisions, particularly tough ones, is to "just decide." Don't agonize over them, don't even think about them too much—just pick one option with little or no thought and move on. Flipping a coin, "eeny meeny miny mo," and "she loves me, she loves me not" with a flower would be examples of this kind of superficial or whimsical method. This approach has a certain appeal, because through it we can avoid the responsibility and hard work of making wise choices.

Some Christians have even tried to "sanctify" this approach by bringing the Bible into it. When in need of guidance, they will close their eyes, let their Bible fall open in front of them, and bring their finger down somewhere on the page. Then they open their eyes and expect that verse to provide them with the guidance they need. As Haddon Robinson explains, however, this doesn't always work out very well:

> There's a story that has lasted a long time not only because of its humor but also because of its insight. It's about a man attempting to discover the mind of God by taking his chances with the Bible. He simply shut his eyes, opened up his Bible, and put his finger on a passage. Opening his eyes, he read this passage from Matthew 27: "Then he went away and

hanged himself." Somehow, the fellow didn't think that gave him any direction for his problem, so he closed his eyes again and opened his Bible to another passage. He looked and read Jesus' statement in Luke 10: "Go and do likewise." That wasn't quite what he was looking for either, so he tried one more time. He shut his eyes, opened his Bible, and read the statement in John 2:5, "Do whatever he tells you."[2]

This approach to decision making is unacceptable for believers, not only because it can yield such bizarre results, but also because the Bible commands against it. Since each of our decisions is so important to God and will have an impact on our lives, Ephesians 5:15–17 says, "Therefore be careful how you walk, not as unwise men, but as wise, making the most of your time, because the days are evil. So then *do not be foolish*, but understand what the will of the Lord is."

A modern synonym for the Greek word translated "foolish" is stupid, and that is an apt description of making decisions based on "chance." It is stupidity. God has given us brains, and he wants us to use them when we make decisions. Most of all, he wants us to exercise biblical wisdom, as we will see in more detail later in this book.

At this point the question might be raised, "Doesn't the Bible talk about casting lots (a practice similar to rolling dice), and didn't the apostles themselves do that?" The answer to both those questions is yes, but that does not necessarily mean we should do it. Let me explain. First, when

Proverbs 16:33 says, "The lot is cast into the lap, but its every decision is from the Lord," it is not commending this method as legitimate, but merely saying that in his sovereignty, God ultimately controls all circumstances, even if they are unfortunate. (For more about this, see chapter 4.) Second, the story in Acts 1:15–26 where the apostles chose a replacement for Judas by lot is part of a narrative account of early church history, and we must be careful not to assume that what happened there is normative for Christians today.[3]

The fact is, the Scriptures never command or even advise us to make decisions by such superficial or whimsical methods. So the team member heading to Russia because he picked a card out of a deck should go back and make his decision in a more biblical manner!

PUTTING GOD IN HIS PLACE

What makes selfish and superficial decisions so wrong is that they "fall short of the glory of God" (Rom. 3:23). We are commanded in 1 Corinthians 10:31, "Whatever you do, do all to the glory of God." So when we give little or no thought to him in our decisions, we are disobeying that command and failing to fulfill the very purpose for our existence. In Isaiah 43:7 God says that mankind has been "created for My glory," and Colossians 1:16 says that "all things have been created by Him and for Him."

You do not exist for the purpose of fulfilling your own

desires and dreams, nor are you a mere collection of random atoms guided by nothing more than blind chance. Rather, as the famous saying goes, God loves you and has a wonderful plan for your life. So therefore what *he wants* should be the most important factor in the choices you make. And that is what it means to bring glory to God in our decisions—to give him that place of importance. Jay Adams explains this concept well:

> The fundamental Greek term for glory is *doxa* ("reputation"). It corresponds closely to the Hebrew word *kabod*, which means "to be heavy." Something glorious is illustrious or has an illustrious reputation because of its weight. As we say, "It carries weight." That this primary Hebrew significance was not to be lost in Greek translation seems clear from Paul's emphasis on it in the phrase, "an eternal weight of glory" (2 Cor. 4:17). . . .
>
> To the humanist, God is a *lightweight:* He is of such little importance . . . that He is not even mentioned. Man is given all the credit. The essence of humanism is that God has been weighed and found wanting. The world, and all that men do in it, is viewed entirely apart from God. Weight is given to man instead."[4]

If we make decisions on the basis of our own selfish desires, or in a careless and sloppy manner, we are essentially agreeing with the humanists that God is not really that important. And if we go to him for help only on the "big" decisions we have to make, we are implying that he is not important in every part of our lives. But when we put God's will above our own in all of our choices, he will be glorified, and we will end up being happier ourselves.

That may seem ironic, because it may not be very enjoyable to submit our will to God's, or to work hard at decision making rather than taking an easy way out. But in the end, we will be glad that we committed ourselves to God, because he rewards those who seek his glory. In fact, this is one of the reasons why he wants us to "do all to the glory of God." John Piper gives us some good insight into this, as he explains how God could be "self-centered" (seeking his own glory), but still be infinitely loving toward his creatures:

> *God is most glorified in us when we are most satisfied in him.* This is perhaps the most important sentence in my theology. If it is true, then it becomes plain why God is loving when he seeks to exalt his glory in my life. For that would mean that he would seek to maximize my satisfaction in him, since he is most glorified in me when I am most satisfied in him. Therefore God's pursuit of his own glory is not at odds with my joy, and that means it is not unkind or unmerciful or unloving of him to seek his glory. In fact it means that the more passionate God is for his

own glory the more passionate he is for my satisfaction in that glory. And therefore God's self-centeredness and God's love soar together.[5]

So for the glory of God, and for your own good, commit yourself to making decisions in a way that honors the Lord, in both your motives and your methods. This is foundational to everything in the rest of this book, because it will only be meaningful and profitable to you if your heart is set on the things that really matter.

A Dragon Tale

One of the most memorable scenes in C. S. Lewis's Chronicles of Narnia occurs in *The Voyage of the Dawn Treader*. Cousin Eustace has unwisely wandered off from the ship's company, into the heart of a mysterious island, where he comes upon the lair of a dead dragon. Running into the cave to escape the harsh rain, he lies down on its floor to take a rest.

> Most of us know what we should expect to find in a dragon's lair, but, as I said before, Eustace had read only the wrong books. They had a lot to say about exports and imports and governments and drains, but they were weak on dragons. That is why he was so puzzled at the surface on which he was lying. Parts of it were too prickly to be stones and too hard to be

thorns, and there seemed to a great many round, flat things, and it all clinked when he moved. There was light enough at the cave's mouth to examine it by. And of course Eustace found it to be what any of us could have told him in advance—treasure. There were crowns (those were the prickly things), coins, rings, bracelets, ingots, cups, plates and gems.

Eustace (unlike most boys) had never thought much of treasure but he saw at once the use it would be in this new world which he had so foolishly stumbled into through the picture in Lucy's bedroom at home. "They don't have any tax here," he said. "And you don't have to give treasure to the government. With some of this stuff I could have quite a decent time here. . . . I wonder how much I can carry? That bracelet now—those things in it are probably diamonds—I'll slip that on my own wrist. Too big, but not if I push it right up here above my elbow. Then fill my pockets with diamonds—that's easier than gold. I wonder when this infernal rain's going to let up?" He got into a less uncomfortable part of the pile, where it was mostly coins, and settled down to wait. But a bad fright, when once it is over, and especially a bad fright following a mountain walk, leaves you very tired. Eustace fell asleep.[6]

He woke up much later to find that he was sleeping between two dragons (or so he thought, because their claws were right next to him). But he then was startled to find that when he made a move to sneak out of the cave, they moved too!

> There was such a clatter and rasping, and clinking of gold, and grinding of stones, as he rushed out of the cave that he thought they were both following him. He daren't look back. He rushed to the pool . . . His idea was to get in the water.
>
> But just as he reached the edge of the pool two things happened. First of all it came over him like a thunderclap that he had been running on all fours—and why on earth had he been doing that? And secondly, as he bent towards the water, he thought for a second that yet another dragon was staring up at him out of the pool. But in an instant he realised the truth. That dragon face in the pool was his own reflection. There was no doubt of it. It moved as he moved: it opened and shut its mouth as he opened and shut his.
>
> He had turned into a dragon while he was asleep. Sleeping on a dragon's hoard with greedy, dragonish thoughts in his heart, he had become a dragon himself.[7]

Eustace is a good illustration of selfishness and carelessness in decision making. But the story also illustrates the worst consequence of bad choices, especially when they are made in the wrong way over and over again: If you practice making your decisions based on selfish motives or superficial methods, you will become a selfish and superficial person. (As we said, we make our decisions, and then our decisions turn around and make us.) Eustace acted like a dragon, and he ended up becoming one. So do not think that you can be foolish in your choices without becoming a fool!

The good news, however, in *The Voyage of the Dawn Treader,* is that the lion Aslan was later able to remove from Eustace his many layers of dragon skin, and then remake him into the person he was meant to be. And the good news for us is that God can take away our wrong approaches to decision making and guide us in the right way. But we must be willing to examine what we have been doing according to the Scriptures with an open mind and heart. And we must be willing to admit where we are wrong, so that God can rearrange us for his glory.

DISCUSSION QUESTIONS

1. Why are you reading this book? What do you hope to learn from it? Is there a specific decision, perhaps a big one, that you are facing right now?

2. Read 1 John 2:15–16. What are examples of how we might base our decisions on the "lust of the flesh"? On the "lust of the eyes"? On the "pride of life"?

3. If you are not sure whether your motives for a decision are sinful, how could you find out?

4. Why do you think God wants us to put serious thought into our decisions, rather than just "letting chance decide"?

5. Give an example of a decision you made that you regret? What is one that you are glad you made?

TWO

SPECIAL REVELATION
OUTSIDE THE BIBLE

This is a prevalent method of decision making in some quarters of Christianity today. When asked how they decided on a particular course of action, some will say, "God told me to do it." And when asked what they mean by that, they will say, "I mean God told me. I heard his voice, as clear as I'm hearing yours now." Or they may have had a vision in which God or one of his angels appeared and spoke to them, like the third member of our make-believe mission team.

What such people are saying, in many cases, is that God told them something besides what he has already told them in the Bible. What they heard from God directly was something more specific and personal than the commands and principles of Scripture. For instance, I once talked with a man who told me that the first time he met a particular woman, he heard a voice from heaven saying, "This is the woman you will marry." I thought to myself that this might have been her mother up above him on a balcony, but he was convinced that it was God speaking to him. He actually did end up marrying that woman, but I hope the experience he had was not the basis for his choice. Despite the amazing coincidence, such an approach would have been unwise.

I say that because no experience we have should ever be given authority in our decision making (see chapter 5), but also because I believe we can say with confidence that God does not speak to us or guide us in that way today. Obviously, God did speak that way (through an unmistakable voice or vision) during Bible times. He did it many times to characters in the Old Testament, like Abraham, Moses, Samuel, Elijah, Isaiah, Ezekiel, and Daniel. He also did it to the New Testament apostles and others in the early church.

But there is a big difference between those ancient believers and us, and that difference is the Bible. They did not have the full written revelation of God as we do. God was still revealing his truth to those people, or to put it another way, revelation was still in progress. But since the completion of the canon of Scripture, God has revealed his truth to us in total. That which he wants us to know, and that which we need to know for our lives here on earth, can be found in its complete form in the pages of the Bible.

God does speak to us today, and he does so practically, personally, and always quite eloquently. But he does so through the written Word of God, made understandable in our hearts and minds by the Holy Spirit of God, and that is the *only* way he speaks today.

THE CASE FOR CESSATION

I realize, as I mentioned earlier, that this perspective regarding the "cessation" of revelation is not shared by many Christians, but I think it is essential as a starting point for making good decisions. If you hope or expect that God will speak to you in the same way he did to some in Bible times, I believe you will be setting yourself up to be seriously disappointed and disillusioned, or at least misled by such "revelations" that under scrutiny cannot be received with full confidence as words from God. Chuck Swindoll provides this warning in his book The Mystery of God's Will:

> . . . this kind of extra-biblical revelation is not only spurious, it's downright dangerous. It invariably leads you astray, away from the truth of God. Your curiosity and your fascination will take over, eclipsing the authority of the Scriptures.
>
> Those who have a high view of biblical revelation, I find, have a very low view of any kind of extra-biblical revelation. Can God do it? Certainly. He is God, and He is able to do whatever He pleases. Does God do it? In all my years of ministry, I've never found a reliable incident of such revelation. On the other hand, I've seen sincere people get into a lot of trouble and confusion because they relied on extra-biblical truth rather than on the Word of God.[1]

Because I believe direct revelation from God outside the Bible should be rejected as a means of guidance (for your good), and because this principle will serve as a foundation for some later discussions in this book, I want to present here some biblical support for the cessation of revelation. The Bible itself teaches its uniqueness as God's only Word for our age, and the following passages are examples of that teaching.

John 16–17

These two chapters contain Jesus' final instructions to his disciples before his death, in the form of teaching in chapter 16 and also the profound intercessory prayer of chapter 17, in which he allowed them to hear his communion with the Father. From the words of our Lord in these passages, an unmistakable doctrine of Scripture emerges. Jesus says, "These things I have spoken to you, that when their hour comes, you may remember that I told you of them. And these things I did not say to you at the beginning, because I was with you" (John 16:4). "Their hour" means the hour of the words, which must be a reference to the approaching time when Matthew, Mark, Luke, and John would write them down for posterity in their gospels.

Then Jesus goes on to predict the inspiration of more books, beyond the gospels, which will complete his Word. John 16:12–15 says, "I have many more things to say to you, but you cannot bear them now. But when He, the Spirit of truth, comes, He will guide you into all the truth;

for He will not speak on His own initiative, but whatever He hears, He will speak; and He will disclose to you what is to come [not future events, but the additional revelation that is to come]. He shall glorify Me; for He shall take of Mine, and shall disclose it to you. All things that the Father has [for believers to know] are Mine; therefore I said, that He takes of Mine, and will disclose it to you." That passage clearly says that the end result of the Spirit's ministry in the apostles would be the revelation of "all truth"—not all the truth that God knows, of course, but all the truth that God wants us to know. Contending that more revelation is necessary after the apostolic age, therefore, is tantamount to saying that the Holy Spirit did not do what he was sent to do.

A few verses later, in John 16:25, Jesus says, "These things I have spoken to you in figurative language; an hour is coming when I will speak no more to you in figurative language, but will tell you plainly of the Father." Again, this is obviously a reference to the apostolic epistles that complete the New Testament, because they clearly have the character of explaining much of what Jesus taught in the Gospels.[2] And in case there might be any doubt that Jesus was talking about a completed written revelation that would be the source of guidance for believers until he returns, he went on to say to his Father in his high priestly prayer, "Sanctify them in the truth; Thy word is truth" (John 17:17).

The point of these passages for our current discussion is that when you put Jesus' words in John 16–17 together with

Hebrews 1:1–2, it becomes clear that Jesus' revelation to the world came through his own words and the words of his apostles, and that revelation was the last word from our Lord until his return.

First Corinthians 13:8–10

While Paul is waxing eloquent about the primacy of love in one of the most famous passages in the Bible, he also says some interesting things about divine revelation:

> Love never fails; but if there are gifts of prophecy, they will be done away; if there are tongues, they will cease; if there is knowledge, it will be done away. For we know in part, and we prophesy in part; but when the perfect comes, the partial will be done away.

Prophecy, tongues, and knowledge are all revelatory gifts. First Corinthians 14 makes clear that both prophecy and tongues were means by which God spoke specific words to the early church (vv. 14–19, 30), and the term "knowledge" is used in 1 Corinthians 12:8–10 in a list of supernatural "sign gifts" that includes tongues and prophecy. We know that the word "knowledge" cannot be used here in the most basic sense of knowing facts, because that ability will never "be done away."

According to Paul, however, this revelatory knowledge will be done away with, as will prophecy and tongues. And he says these gifts will come to an end when the complete revelation comes. (The Greek word translated "perfect" is *telion*, which often means "complete," as opposed to partial.) Some commentators have suggested that the "perfect" or "complete" is the eternal state, but it seems more likely that it is a reference to the completed canon of Scripture.[3] Paul knew that when the Bible was completed, there would be no need for any further revelation, and therefore no need for the revelatory gifts.

Ephesians 2:20

Here Paul says that the church is being "built upon the foundation of the apostles and prophets, Christ Jesus Himself being the corner stone." The apostles and prophets were the instruments of God's revelation in the early church, and of course Christ Jesus himself was the very Word of God, revealing the Father to us. And according to this verse, their revelatory work was foundational, rather than ongoing. As Richard Gaffin writes,

> The foundation in view is finished; it is a historically completed entity. When a builder knows what he is doing (as we may assume God does in this instance!) the foundation is poured once at the beginning of the project; it doesn't need to be repeatedly relaid. The foundation's completion is followed by the ongoing work of building the superstructure on that foundation, until the building's

completion. From our vantage point today, we are in the period of the superstructure; laying the foundation is done, a thing of the past.[4]

There are no more apostles or prophets today—those offices were intended only for the early, foundational era when the old covenant community of Israel was developing into the new covenant church (and the latter was emerging from the former). And since that transition was completed and the Bible has been finished (cf. Dan. 9:24 and Rev. 22:18–19), there is no longer any need for new revelation that was delivered by the apostles and prophets.[5] The foundation has already been laid, and our job is simply to build our lives in conformity to the Word that has already been revealed.

Second Timothy 3:16–17

This passage tells us why there was no need for further revelation after the canon of Scripture was closed. God put his book together in such a way that it would have everything we need for life and godliness (2 Pet. 1:3). Paul writes, "All Scripture is inspired by God and profitable for teaching, for reproof, for correction, for training in righteousness; that the man of God may be adequate, equipped for every good work." "Adequate" means "having everything we need," of course, and the Greek word translated "equipped" (*exertismenos*) also carries with it the idea of completeness—it could be translated "fully or totally equipped." As John Calvin wrote, in his commentary on this verse:

> Perfect means here a blameless person, one in whom there is nothing defective; for he asserts absolutely, that the Scripture is sufficient for perfection. Accordingly, he who is not satisfied with Scripture desires to be wiser than is either proper or desirable.[6]

Hebrews 1:1–2 and 2:3–4

The first of these passages contains a definitive statement that the words of Jesus are the final words from God for the church age:

> God, after He spoke long ago to the fathers in the prophets in many portions and in many ways, in these last days has spoken to us in His Son, whom He appointed heir of all things, through whom also He made the world.

Notice also that according to this passage, special revelation was not normative for all of God's people at all times in history. In other words, though God did speak in a voice or vision to some believers at some times, there were many other times when no one heard his voice directly. So most believers throughout history have had to seek God's guidance from the Scriptures they possessed, which were the written records of what he had said in a former time. God's revelation was a series of stops and starts throughout the history of his people Israel, and Hebrews 1 says the last start and the final stop has taken place in Jesus Christ.

The passage in Hebrews 2 tells us, as we learned from John 16–17, that the Word of Christ also included the words of his apostles. In other words, the writing ministry of the apostles in the years following Christ's ascension was the completion of his revelation to the world:

> How shall we escape if we neglect so great a salvation? After it was at the first spoken through the Lord, it was confirmed to us by those who heard, God also bearing witness with them, both by signs and wonders and by various miracles and by gifts of the Holy Spirit according to His own will.

Second Peter 1:19

After describing the wonders of his greatest spiritual experience (he witnessed the transfiguration of Christ), Peter writes, "We have the prophetic word made more sure, to which you do well to pay attention as to a lamp shining in a dark place, until the day dawns and the morning star arises in your hearts." What was the prophetic word that was even more reliable than his rapturous experience on the mountain? The reference to a lamp provides a hint (see Psalm 119:105), but then in verses 20–21 Peter makes it clear that he is talking about the written Word of God:

> But know this first of all, that no prophecy of Scrip-
> ture is a matter of one's own interpretation, for no
> prophecy was ever made by an act of human will,
> but men moved by the Holy Spirit spoke from God.

Notice that verse 19 also contains a strong implication of the finality of New Testament revelation for the church age. Peter says the light of Scripture will be your source of guidance "until the day dawns and the morning star arises." Assuming this is a reference to the Second Coming of Christ, it becomes clear that God intended the Bible to be all we need until he returns.

Jude 3

In the second-to-last book of the Bible, we are told to "contend earnestly for the faith which was once for all delivered to the saints." Apparently some false teachers in the early church were claiming that they had new revelation beyond the apostolic witness and its inspired Scriptures. Jude wanted to make sure that his readers knew that God's revelation was being delivered to the church "once for all" (Gk. *hapax*), which meant it had definite boundaries and would be completed shortly.[7] About this verse, Jay Adams writes,

> The faith had been given to the saints in a full and
> final way. Nothing more need be added; none dare
> say that God had given an insufficient revelation to

His people. Yet you will discover [people] who are looking for "something more." There is nothing more to be found. What they need is not something more, but more of the something that they already have in Christ. . . . Whenever [someone] refers to "something more" than that which is a part of the deposit of the faith now found in the Bible alone, warn him that what he is playing around with is dangerous because, in reality, it isn't something more but something *different*. Whatever is added to the once-for-all delivered deposit of the faith always becomes more important than the truths contained in that deposit itself."[8]

Revelation 22:18

In the last book of the Bible, and in the last paragraph of the Bible (facts that could hardly be coincidental), the apostle John says, "I testify to everyone who hears the words of the prophecy of this book: if anyone adds to them, God shall add to him the plagues which are written in this book." As O. Palmer Robertson writes in his excellent book *The Final Word*,

This final "Do not add" obviously applies first to the book of Revelation written under God's inspiration by the apostle John himself. To the prophecy of this book nothing is to be added, and from the book of this prophecy nothing is to be taken away. But the book of Revelation holds a unique position in the authoritative revelations from God. Presenting Christ as he will be seen again only when he returns in glory, its admonition that no one must presume to add excludes any and all pretensions to further revelations.[9]

EXTRABIBLICAL REVELATION: MORE OR LESS?

Although the preceding passages multiply support for the idea that God does not speak outside of the Scriptures today, many Christians find this thought utterly unacceptable. Perhaps the biggest reason is that if they admit that special revelation has ceased, they will be saying goodbye to a close friend. The voices they have heard and the visions they have received from God and his angels are an integral part of their Christian experiences, and without them they think that God would be too distant and uninvolved in their lives. But by seeking guidance through such means, I fear that they are actually missing some of the greatest blessings God has for them in the wisdom of his Word.

Robertson again speaks appropriately to this matter in the conclusion of his book:

Great benefits come to God's people if they are willing to take seriously the fact that the "final revelation" has come in the Christ of the Scriptures. Far from hindering enthusiasm and a sense of the immediacy of God's presence in their midst, faith in the sufficiency of Scripture will move them to serve him with the full vigour of their beings. It must not be forgotten how the resurrected Christ stirred the hearts of his depressed disciples. The Gospel of Luke explains that Jesus enlivened his followers by opening to them the Scriptures. Beginning with Moses and all the prophets, he explained to them what was said in all the Scriptures concerning himself (Luke 24:27). Why? Why did the resurrected Christ speak to them in this way? Why did he not simply give to them a new revelation?

The resurrected Jesus opened the Scriptures to them because that would be the way by which spiritual life would be sustained for them from that point on. As a consequence of his opening the Scriptures, their hearts burned within them (Luke 24:32). The same principle has continued through all the ages. As the resurrected Christ through his Spirit opens the Scriptures to his people, their hearts have burned within them. Much greater than depending on the stimulus of new revelations of the Spirit is living out of the sufficiency of the final word as it is found in the Christ of the Scriptures.

And why not both? Why not the illumination of Scripture coupled with new revelations of the Spirit? Simply because if you declare a need for both, you have implied the insufficiency of the one. You have placed yourself back in the framework of the old covenant, in a time when new revelations were required because of the incompleteness of the old. But Christ is the final word. No further word for the redemption of men in the present age is needed.[10]

And no further word is needed for their guidance, either. In fact, I would suggest that we are actually much better off than the people in ancient times who received direct revelation from God. It was a sign of weakness, not of strength, that they needed such words from God, because they did not yet have his full written revelation. And they received their revelation only periodically, whereas we have it at our fingertips at all times. They had to merely hope that God *might* provide guidance for a particular decision, but we know that he already has provided it in a completed, sufficient Bible. So the fact that God speaks today only through his Word is a blessing, not a handicap.

What this all means in regard to our topic is that when you are making decisions, you should not be trying to get more information from God than he has given to you in the Scriptures. You certainly can and will discover truth and direction in his Word that you have never seen before, and you certainly will learn to apply his scriptural truth in new ways as you go about making decisions. But you should not in any way be seeking new specific or personal revelation from God.

As Robertson implied, even the work of the Holy Spirit (who indwells believers) is not to reveal new truth to us, but to illumine our hearts and minds to the truth already revealed in Scripture, to cause us to conform more and more to that truth, and to guide us in the process of applying that truth with godly wisdom (Rom. 8:14; 1 Cor. 2; 2 Cor. 3:18; Gal. 5:18). In fact, the ministry of the Spirit of God is inextricably linked to the Word of God—to the extent that the two are often interchangeable in Scripture. For instance, Ephesians 5:18 and Colossians 3:16 are parallel verses in parallel books. One says, "Be filled with the Spirit," and the other says, "Let the Word of Christ richly dwell within you" (cf. Heb. 3:7; 2 Pet. 1:20–21).

An adaptation of a rather fanciful and hypothetical story told by Haddon Robinson will serve as a good conclusion to this discussion of special revelation outside the Bible:

Suppose that because of the constant prayers of his people seeking revelation ("Lord, speak to us!"), somehow Jesus is coaxed down from heaven to appear briefly, before his Second Coming (which would then have to be his Third Coming!). He agrees to make a short appearance at a particular location at a particular time, and all corners of the press begin a mad scramble to get their cameras there—because when Jesus appears, he has promised that he will tell everyone in the world exactly what God wants us to know and do at the dawn of the third millennium.

As the crowds gasp, and the cameras whir, Jesus steps up to the microphone and holds up a Bible.

"I have already told you," he says. "I have given you my Word, which contains all you need to know for faith, godliness, and guidance. I have also given you my Spirit to help you understand the Word and apply it in your life. If you want to do what I want you to do in every decision of your life, study this book and live out its principles by the power of the Spirit."

Then he vanishes.

I hope you will never need such a reminder, because you will always be seeking your guidance from inside the Bible rather than outside of it.

DISCUSSION QUESTIONS

1. Is the idea that God speaks *only* in the Bible a new one to you? What understanding of God's revelation have you had up to this point?

2. Which passage discussed in "The Case for Cessation" did you think was the most persuasive? Explain how that passage relates to the issue of how God speaks to us today.

3. When God spoke to people verbally in Bible times, did they have difficulty determining whether it was his voice? How does this compare to the practice of Christians today who say, "God told me . . ."?

4. If God's Word is found only in the Bible today, do you think we are better off than those in ancient times who literally heard his voice? Why or why not?

5. How do you think this chapter applies to the way you make decisions?

THREE

SUPERNATURAL SIGNS

This fourth and final "road to nowhere" is closely related to the previous one, because in the context of decision making, supernatural signs are a form of fresh revelation from God. Someone cannot decide which way to go, so God sends him a miraculous event to show him what he should do, like the missions team member who saw Dan Rather doing the news in Russian. This kind of "sign" is basically the equivalent of God speaking verbally on the matter. The difference between the two could be likened to the difference between saying "Go to the right" and pointing to the right. Either way, the source of the guidance is extrabiblical revelation.

PUTTING OUT A FLEECE

Miraculous signs were used as a method of decision making by some characters in the Bible. The classic example is Gideon, one of the leaders in Israel in the book of

Judges. In Judges 6:16, God had told Gideon that he would deliver Israel from the Midianites, if Gideon would simply follow his commands. But as the day of battle approached, Gideon started to get cold feet. Judges 6:36–40 tells us that he needed a sign from God (not once, but twice) before he would be willing to risk his neck:

> Then Gideon said to God, "If Thou wilt deliver Israel through me, as Thou hast spoken, behold, I will put a fleece of wool on the threshing floor. If there is dew on the fleece only, and it is dry on all the ground, then I will know that Thou wilt deliver Israel through me, as Thou hast spoken." And it was so. When he arose early the next morning and squeezed the fleece, he drained the dew from the fleece, a bowl full of water. Then Gideon said to God, "Do not let Thine anger burn against me that I may speak once more; please let me make a test once more with the fleece, let it now be dry only on the fleece, and let there be dew on all the ground." And God did so that night; for it was dry only on the fleece, and dew was on all the ground.

This story has given rise to a prevalent method of decision making called "putting out a fleece." Someone asks God for a supernatural sign to determine or affirm a particular decision. "Lord, if there is an earthquake today, I'll know that you want me to ask her out." Or perhaps the "sign" may be something much less earth-shaking: "Streetlights have been blinking out when I drive by them, so I think God is telling me to get a new car." But there are at least two big problems with seeking God's guidance in this way.

First, as with Gideon, this approach can easily be a cloak for our own sinfulness (or stupidity). Gideon had already received a clear word from the Lord that he would win the battle—he asked for a sign because he lacked faith and was hoping he could get out of what he knew God wanted him to do. So rather than providing a paradigm for Christians to follow, Gideon is a profound example of how not to make decisions! But unfortunately, many Christians have followed his example, and many have done so with the same wrong motives. God has spoken clearly about something in his Word, but they ignore it, or refuse to discover it through study and counsel, and then they say, "God hasn't shown me." A woman committing adultery, for instance, says "I prayed to God to show me if I'm wrong, but he didn't." She is waiting for a sign before she will do what God has commanded her to do, or before she will look to see what the Word says to do.

If we do that, we become like the man in the old joke who sits on his roof with flood waters rising all around him, praying "Lord, please deliver me." One of his neighbors rows by in a little boat, yelling to him to get in and flee to safety, but he says, "No thank you, the Lord will deliver me." Then, as the water begins to cover his feet, a Coast Guard cutter swings by, its crew shouting, "Come on, buddy, you're gonna die!" Again he says, "Go on—the Lord will deliver me." Finally, as the water engulfs his chest and then his chin, a rescue helicopter lowers a ladder right next to his head. He refuses to take it, however, and from beneath the water he gurgles, with his last breath, "The Lord will deliver me." Shortly after, he reaches the pearly gates and is granted an audience with the Lord, to whom he says indignantly, "Why didn't you save me?!" The Lord replies, "I sent you two boats and a helicopter—what more do you want?!"

We can be like that man—sitting on the sinking house of our sin or indifference, waiting for God to show us his will when he already has in the Scriptures. Jesus referred to this ungodly tendency when he said, "An evil and adulterous generation seeks after a sign" (Matt. 16:4). Not content with the wisdom of the Word and the presence of the Spirit, we look for "something more."

SIGNS OF THE TIMES

Although Gideon and others in the Bible sought supernatural signs for illegitimate motives, there were other people who did receive real guidance from the Lord through them. A good example is the pillar of cloud by day and the pillar of fire by night that God used to tell the Israelites which way they should go as they wandered in the wilderness. But the problem with seeking such miracles for guidance today, however, is that God doesn't give them anymore. There are no pillars of cloud and fire, no wet and dry fleeces, or anything even similar today. Supernatural signs are a thing of the past, and perhaps a thing of the future, but in the present they are not happening.

Before I go on to explain why that is true, let me clarify what I mean by "supernatural signs," so there will be no confusion. When I speak of "signs," I am not referring to the amazing things that happen every day in the world by God's power, such as the universe holding together, the sick being healed in mysterious ways through prayers, or people being born again by the Spirit of God. Nor am I referring to the "amazing coincidences" that happen every day by God's providence, such as a believer escaping death in a car accident by mere inches or an anonymous check arriving for the exact amount needed. What I mean by "supernatural signs" is what the New Testament means when it uses words like "signs, wonders, and miracles" (Heb. 2:4). These are highly notable works of God that are unusual even for him, such as raising the dead, parting a sea, and walking on water. Etymologically, the word "supernatural" does not merely mean "spiritual in nature," but "beyond the normal nature of things." And when the Bible talks about signs, wonders, and miracles, it is talking about special events that go beyond the normal ways God uses his power in the world. They are something different than the typical way our Lord works, because they are designed to get everyone's attention and point to something (that's why they are called "signs").

By understanding the unique nature of such miracles, and the special purposes God had for them, we can see why they are no longer necessary today. Two of the primary purposes for these signs linked them inextricably to special revelation. First, supernatural signs themselves were a means of special revelation. As I mentioned earlier, they were one of God's ways of telling people what they should do, such as the pillars in the wilderness ("Go that way") or Gideon's fleeces ("Yes, you will win the battle!"). But also, supernatural signs were a validation of those who brought special revelation. At the selected times in history when God wanted to reveal new parts of the Bible, he sent miracles to surround the people who spoke for him, so others would know that they had divine authority to reveal and record God's Word.

Hebrews 2:3–4 teaches this purpose for supernatural signs as clearly as possible: "How shall we escape if we neglect so great a salvation? After it was at the first spoken through the Lord, it was confirmed to us by those who heard [the apostles and other men close to them], God also bearing witness with them, both by signs and wonders and by various miracles and by gifts of the Holy Spirit according to His own will." Also notice Paul's words in 2 Corinthians 12:12, when he is trying to convince the church that the words he writes are the words of God: "The signs of a true apostle were performed among you with all perseverance, by signs and wonders and miracles" (cf. Acts 2:22).

The whole point of a sign is to indicate the uniqueness of someone or something. That someone or something in the Scriptures is the people who spoke for God and the writings they composed for God. Now that the Bible is complete, now that God has spoken (Heb. 1:2; Jude 3), there is no longer any need for supernatural signs like those that took place while the Word was being written.

When we understand the revelational purposes of miracles, we should expect them to have ceased when revelation ceased. And they did. Supernatural signs like those that happened in Bible times simply do not occur today, as mere observation confirms. When is the last time you turned on the news and saw camera footage of a man tapping his staff on Lake Michigan and watching it separate before him, clearing a dry path to the other side? When have you read in a credible newspaper (not the supermarket tabloids) that a prophet of God like Elijah prayed to God and brought down a barrage of flame from the clouds, consuming cultic leaders in a scene like the end of *Raiders of the Lost Ark*? And when have you seen one of those "faith healers" walking through the halls of a hospital, immediately releasing everyone from their maladies, much less visiting the morgue or cemetery and raising someone from the dead?[1]

Someone may say, "I did hear of things like that happening in healing crusades, or among the Indians down in South America," or something similar. But I would suggest that the fact that such "miracles" are disputed by so many proves that they are not the biblical kind. When miracles happened in the Bible, no one denied that they were miracles, nor did anyone deny that they happened. Even the hardened Pharisees, who would have welcomed any reason to explain away the miracles of Christ, could not deny that he did them. Instead, the enemies of our Lord had to resort to claiming that he did what he did by the power of Satan (Matt. 12:24).

Because supernatural signs are tied so closely to special revelation, asking God to guide you by them is no more valid than asking him to speak to you audibly. In order to make good decisions, you need to avoid these roads to nowhere and walk the path of biblical wisdom.

DISCUSSION QUESTIONS

1. Have you ever made a decision based on a "sign"? How did it turn out?
2. Some have said that looking for a sign from God is a lazy way of making decisions. What do you think?
3. Is there a difference between the way the Bible uses the word "miracles" and the way Christians today tend to use it?
4. When people believe that God does the same kinds of miracles today that he did in biblical times, how do they explain that so many of the ones mentioned in the Bible are not happening (such as raising the dead, fire from heaven, walking on water, etc.)?
5. What verses in Scripture would you show people if they asked about the *purpose* of miracles? In other words, why did miracles happen, according to the Bible?

FOUR

THE WILL OF GOD

The first few chapters of this book discussed some entirely erroneous approaches to decision making, and now we will begin to consider some ideas that contain truth, but are often misunderstood and misapplied. One such idea is reflected in some of the most common terminology heard among Christians in the context of decision making. They are often heard saying things like this: "I'm trying to find the will of God," or "I just want to do whatever God's will is." Those statements reflect a commendable attitude (desiring to please God), but they are often based on a misunderstanding of what the Bible means when it talks about "the will of God."

For example, imagine a fifth member of our fictional summer missions team to Russia. When asked the reason why she is going, she says, "God revealed to me that it was his will, and I would be out of the will of God if I stayed home." She seems to have the best motives for her choice, but based on her reasons, it may not actually be the best decision for her to make. She has some wrong conceptions in her mind about the will of God that could be leading her astray. At the end of this chapter we will return to her, and hopefully by then you will be able to discern the errors in her thinking. But to get there, we have to first do some serious study and thinking to understand what "the will of God" is according to the Scriptures.

WHICH WILL OF GOD?

The first thing you need to understand is that the Bible uses the terminology "will of God" to express two different concepts.[1] One is commonly called the sovereign will of God (also known as the "secret" or "decretive" will). The other is called the moral will (also known as the "revealed" or "preceptive" will). These basic categorizations of the biblical data related to God's will have been articulated throughout the history of Christian theology (though sometimes in different words), and I believe they accurately reflect what the Bible teaches. I also think this understanding of the two senses of the term is absolutely essential to think clearly and avoid confusion in our approach to making decisions.

The sovereign will of God is his pre-ordained purpose—whatever he has planned to occur in the universe and in our lives. It is called "secret" because we do not and cannot know anything he has planned before it actually happens (with the exception of prophecies of future events). And the term "decretive" is an old one that comes from the idea of God's "decree," summarized well by the Westminster Confession of Faith, written in 1648:

> God from all eternity, did, by the most wise and holy counsel of His own will, freely, and unchange-ably ordain whatsoever comes to pass: yet so, as thereby neither is God the author of sin, nor is vio-lence offered to the will of the creatures. (III, 1)

The Lord himself describes his sovereign will in Isaiah 46:9–11: "I am God, and there is no other; I am God, and there is no one like Me, declaring the end from the begin-ning and from ancient times things which have not been done, saying, 'My purpose will be established, and I will ac-complish all My good pleasure; calling a bird of prey from the east, the man of My purpose from a far country. Truly I have spoken; truly I will bring it to pass. I have planned it, surely I will do it.' " Notice from that passage that God's sovereign will is exhaustive and comprehensive, it extends even to the smallest details, such as where a bird flies, and even to the choices of individual people (v. 11).

The sovereign plan of God also extends to bad things that happen, such as natural disasters and the evil that men do. Consider these verses:

> That men may know from the rising to the setting of the sun that there is no one besides Me. I am the

Lord, and there is no other, the One forming light and creating darkness, causing well-being and creating calamity; I am the Lord who does all these. (Isa. 45:6–7)

Men of Israel, listen to these words: Jesus the Nazarene, a man attested to you by God with miracles and wonders and signs which God performed through Him in your midst, just as you yourselves know—this Man, delivered up by the predetermined plan and foreknowledge of God, you nailed to a cross by the hands of godless men and put Him to death. (Acts 2:22–23)

For truly in this city there were gathered together against Thy holy servant Jesus, whom Thou didst anoint, both Herod and Pontius Pilate, along with the Gentiles and the peoples of Israel, to do whatever Thy hand and Thy purpose predestined to occur. (Acts 4:27–28)

Ephesians 1:11 summarizes this concept well when it says that believers have been "predestined according to His purpose who works all things after the counsel of His will." That verse uses three different Greek words to express the idea of God's sovereign plan: *prothesis* ("purpose" or "intention"), *boule* ("counsel" or "determination"), and *thelo* ("will" or "desire"). It may be helpful to note, for those who like to look further into the original languages of Scripture, that the first two words, in both their noun and verb forms, are always used of an intention or decision, but never of a mere desire. So when you see those two Greek terms used in relation to God, you can assume that they are speaking of his sovereign will.[2] *Thelo,* on the other hand, is a broader term that can refer to either a determination or a desire, depending on the context.[3]

The moral will of God, on the other hand, is not what he has planned to occur, but what he commands and what brings him pleasure. Whereas the sovereign will includes everything that happens, the moral will expresses what should happen. It is the will that God has made known to his creatures through his Word, therefore it is also called the "revealed will." And the older term "preceptive" comes from the idea of God's "precepts," or the instructions he has given us in the Bible.

We find this meaning of the will of God all throughout Scripture, but here are a few examples:

I delight to do *Thy will,* O my God; Thy Law is within my heart. (Psalm 40:8)

But if you bear the name "Jew," and rely upon the Law, and boast in God, and know *His will,* and approve the things that are essential, being instructed out of the Law. (Rom. 2:17–18)

So then do not be foolish, but understand what *the will of the Lord* is.* (Eph. 5:17)

For this reason also, since the day we heard of it, we have not ceased to pray for you and to ask that you may be filled with the knowledge of *His will* in all spiritual wisdom and understanding, so that you may walk in a manner worthy of the Lord, to please Him in all respects, bearing fruit in every good work and increasing in the knowledge of God. (Col. 1:9–10)

Those passages speak of the will of God as something that is revealed in the Scriptures, and something that we can "understand" and "know." This is markedly different from the sovereign will that cannot be known before it happens (Prov. 20:24; Deut. 29:29). And another difference between the two is that the sovereign will always comes to pass exactly as God has planned (Rom. 9:19; Heb. 6:17), but the moral will can be disobeyed by men, and often is (1 Thess. 4:3, 5:18). So there are clearly two senses to the idea of "the will of God," and we see them both illustrated repeatedly in the stories of the Bible.

For example, take the story of Joseph in Genesis, chapters 37–50. His jealous brothers made a choice to sell him into slavery, and that decision clearly violated the moral or revealed will of God. God had told them in his Word that they should love rather than hate, and that they should care for their brother rather than hurt him. But they disobeyed God, and in that sense his will was not done. But notice what Joseph said to his brothers after he endured slavery and prison, only to rise to the position of second-in-command in Egypt:

> God sent me before you to preserve for you a remnant in the earth, and to keep you alive by a great deliverance. Now, therefore, *it was not you who sent me here, but God;* and He has made me a father to Pharaoh and lord of all his household and ruler over all the land of Egypt. (Gen. 45:7–8)

> And as for you, you meant evil against me, but God *meant it for good* in order to bring about this present result, to preserve many people alive. (Gen. 50:20)

Joseph understood that although his brothers' actions were in violation of the moral will of God, they fit squarely within his sovereign will. And this was the case also with the murder of Jesus Christ, mentioned in the verses above from the book of Acts. The Jews and Romans defied the revealed will of God by killing the Messiah (and they later suffered the consequences for such a heinous act). But on the other hand, the crucifixion of Christ was exactly what needed to happen for God's eternal purposes to be accomplished.

A verse that mentions both meanings of the "will of God" is Deuteronomy 29:29 and therefore would be a good one for you to memorize. In the context before that verse, God tells the people of Israel that sometime in the future, they would forsake his covenant and be cursed for doing so.

No doubt they were wondering when this might happen, and perhaps they were even paralyzed with fear at the thought of it. So Moses elucidates for them the relationship of God's sovereignty to human responsibility: "The secret things belong to the Lord our God, but the things revealed belong to us and to our sons forever, that we may observe all the words of this law."

Basically, Moses told them not to worry about God's sovereign plan, but rather to worry about what they should be doing. The details of God's sovereign plan, such as the "when" of future prophecy, are "secret things" that only God knows. But "the things revealed" in his Word should be the focus and basis of our decisions. Moses emphasizes this point a few verses later in Deuteronomy 30:10–14:

> If you obey the Lord your God to keep His commandments and His statutes which are written in this book of the law, if you turn to the Lord your God with all your heart and soul. For this commandment which I command you today is not too difficult for you, nor is it out of reach. It is not in heaven, that you should say, "Who will go up to heaven for us to get it for us and make us hear it, that we may observe it?" Nor is it beyond the sea, that you should say, "Who will cross the sea for us to get it for us and make us hear it, that we may observe it?" But the word is very near you, in your mouth and in your heart, that you may observe it.

This is where all our discussion about the "will of God" in Scripture becomes very practical for our decision making. As Moses said to the people of Israel, we should not be concerned with the sovereign will of God when we face a decision (except that we need to be ready to accept whatever the Lord has planned). The guidance we need for our choices does not have to be somehow mined from the mysterious and unknowable plan devised among the Holy Trinity in eternity past. Rather it is a relatively simple process of finding out what the Bible says and doing it. But unfortunately many Christians are looking for God to tell them the specifics of his plan before they make a decision. They are not content to make their choices based on the principles in the revealed Word, but want God to give them some more specific information, direction, or guidance.

A SPIRITUAL "WILD GOOSE CHASE"

I am convinced that much of the confusion and frustration experienced by Christians who are "seeking the will of God" comes from failing to distinguish between the sovereign and moral will. R. C. Sproul addresses this problem in his book *Can I Know God's Will?*:

> The practical question of how we know the will of God for our lives cannot be solved with any degree of accuracy unless we have some prior understanding of the will of God in general. Without the distinc-

tions we have made, our pursuit of the will of God can plunge us into hopeless confusion and consternation. When we seek the will of God, we must first ask ourselves which will we are seeking to discover.

If our quest is to penetrate the hidden aspects of His will, then we have embarked on a fool's errand. We are trying the impossible and chasing the untouchable. Such a quest is not only an act of foolishness, but also an act of presumption. There is a very real sense in which the secret will of the secret counsel of God is none of our business and is off limits to our speculative investigations.

Untold evils have been perpetrated upon the church and upon God's people by unscrupulous theologians who have sought to correct or to supplant the clear and plain teaching of sacred Scripture by doctrines and theories based on speculation alone. The business of searching out the mind of God where God has remained silent is dangerous business indeed. Luther put it this way, "We must keep in view His Word and leave alone His inscrutable will; for it is by His Word and not by His inscrutable will that we must be guided."[4]

I believe Sproul and Luther are right, and let me put it in another way that should illustrate the "foolishness" they speak of. Imagine if Joseph's brothers were deciding whether to sell him into slavery, and one said, "Let's do it,

because maybe he will end up surviving, becoming power-
ful in another country, and helping us someday." Or what if
the Jews and Romans somehow knew that it was God's plan
for Jesus to die, so they went ahead and killed him to "fulfill God's plan." Would they have been right in doing so?
The answer is no, and that illustrates why we should not be
seeking for God to reveal the details of his sovereign will to
us ahead of time, as a source of guidance. Because if we
could somehow use his sovereign will as a basis for our decisions, it would sometimes lead us right into sin (because
God has chosen to allow sin)! And that would contradict
everything the Lord has told us about our responsibility to
make the right choices according to his Word. So we are
left with hopeless confusion.

But remember Deuteronomy 29:29 ("The secret things
belong to the Lord our God, but the things revealed belong
to us . . .") and you will have a clearer understanding of the
will of God and how it relates to your decisions. God has a
sovereign will that is a mystery to us, and this secret plan
includes everything that happens, even our wrong choices.
But God reveals to us his moral will in Scripture, and we
have the privilege of making our choices based on that revelation, incurring blessing or discipline depending on how
we choose. From God's perspective, he knows all our
choices ahead of time and actually has planned for us to
make them. But from our perspective, we do not know his
plan until it happens, so it is our responsibility to make our
decisions based on the commands and principles revealed

in his Word. It is important to know that God is ultimately in control of our decisions, because then we will not become proud if we make good ones, or too depressed if we make bad ones (because he can still work them for good). But we also need to recognize our responsibility to choose, because if we do not we will be frozen into sinful inaction. To put it another way, our decisions are definitely a part of God's plan, but he does not make them for us.

We should simply accept God's sovereign will and choose according to his moral will, but many Christians have hopelessly muddled their decision-making process by inventing another meaning for the "will of God," and making that wrong concept the basis for their decisions. Let me explain how this happens. Many Christians think that "God has a unique individual plan for my life, which includes every specific detail." So far so good, but then they say, "I've got to find out what that will is and decide to do it, or else I will be out of God's will." Single people, for instance, are looking for "The One" God has planned for them to marry, and expecting God to reveal who that "One" is before they get married. And if they do not choose the right "One," then they fear they will be "out of the will of God," or be settling for "God's second best."[5]

This thinking lies behind much of the terminology used by Christians in conversations, and also in books and other forms of teaching about guidance and the will of God. People talk about "discerning God's will," "finding God's will," "discovering God's will," and "knowing the will of the

Lord." And usually when they use this kind of terminology, they are not thinking of the sovereign will of God or the moral will of God, but a third concept different from both of them. It has sometimes been called "the individual will of God," "the perfect will of God," or "the center of God's will." But the idea is always the same: a unique and specific plan that God has for every life, which he is trying to communicate to us for our guidance.

God does have a unique and specific plan for every life, as we have learned, but that is his sovereign will, which is "secret" and cannot be known ahead of time for the purposes of guidance. And the moral will, which is provided for our guidance, contains general commands and principles rather than specific, personal details. This third idea, of an "individual will" different from the sovereign will and more specific than the moral will, is not a biblical concept, as Dr. James Petty explains:

> The phrase "will of God" is simply not used in this sense of an idealized personal plan that forms a pattern for decision making. This supposed "individual will" is not God's sovereign will, which is behind providence, nor is it the revealed will of God in Scripture. It is something in between these two and separate from them. The passages that are cited (Col. 1:9; 4:12; Rom. 12:2; Eph. 5:17; 6:6), all actually refer to God's will as revealed in his commandments and applied to our lives. So advocates of this

view are using a category that is not introduced in Scripture—a big problem![6]

Another problem with this understanding of the will of God is that those who seek it must go beyond Scripture as their source of divine revelation. Since they are often looking for guidance about specific details that are not addressed in the Bible, they listen for God to "speak" to them about those details in some way other than the Bible. This may be through feelings, impressions, promptings, circumstances, prayer, or other means. And in this way, even many Christians who would not consider themselves "charismatic" end up following the same basic approach as those who claim to hear the voice of God through prophecy, tongues, and visions. Their desire to "find the will of God" (in the wrong sense) inevitably leads them away from the written Word of God as the primary source of direction.

GOD'S WILL AND PERSONAL HYGIENE

To understand how decision making is affected by a biblical understanding of the will of God, and also by common misunderstandings, consider the following example.

Brushing my teeth daily, or at least regularly, seems to be a clear moral and biblical obligation for me. God tells me to love my wife, not to be rude to others, and not to bring reproach upon myself as a pastor! But whether I brush an extra time or two each day, and what kind of toothpaste

I use, clearly seem to be matters of wisdom (in that those choices may affect my later health and appearance in some way). When deciding on those issues, I have moved into a realm of freedom, where I could choose any one of several options and still be within God's will. (That is definitely the case when I get to issues like brushing up or down or sideways, which bathroom I use, what color brush, and so on.)

Now think about this: God may cause me to do one or more of those little things not addressed in his Word, in order to accomplish his sovereign plan. For instance, suppose that one morning I find that the floor is sticky in my bathroom, so I take my toothbrush and toothpaste over to our second bathroom to avoid standing on it. While I am there, the light bulb above the sink burns out. So that night I stop by the hardware store to buy one on my way home from work, and by doing so I miss being in a car accident that would have killed me if I had gone straight home. That sort of thing can happen, and in fact it does all the time! The Bible says that "God causes all things to work together" (Rom. 8:28), even the smallest details. But we cannot understand all the hows and whys of his sovereign will, and it is also not our responsibility to ascertain it before it happens.

Can you imagine if every morning I stood there frozen into inaction wondering, "Is it God's will for me to use this bathroom or the other one (because my life may depend on it)?" Or what if I prayed, "Please God, reveal your will to me about which direction I should brush this morning?" But those are the kinds of things I would do if I really believed that God had an "individual will" for every choice that he wants me to discover, or if I had to find the "dot" in the center of God's will, as some have said. To be consistent, I would have to "seek God's will" for the most insignificant choices. And I would also have to be looking for special revelation outside of Scripture constantly, because the Bible does not speak to many such choices. In regard to matters like brushing my teeth, it makes much more sense to understand that as long as I do not violate the moral will of God in any way, I have freedom to choose on the basis of wisdom and desire (see chapters 9–10). And whatever happens as a result of my choices is a part of God's sovereign plan, designed with my best in mind. So I do not have to worry about "missing the will of God" in any sense.

Remember the fifth missions trip member who said, "I am going because God revealed to me that it was his will" (see page 43)? So far so good, if she meant that her going was consistent with God's Word (the Great Commission, for instance). But the rest of her words probably reveal a misunderstanding: "And I would be out of the will of God if I stayed home." If she means that staying home would have violated a scriptural command or principle, then she would indeed be "out of the will of God" and in need of repentance. But more likely she is saying that God told her "I want you to go," perhaps not verbally, but through other ways like feelings, impressions, or circumstances. She was looking for God to speak to this specific choice, and she thinks that she has heard from God.

But maybe it would be *wiser* for her to stay home (if she is in debt, for instance), or maybe she wants to stay home for good reasons and is feeling pressure from others to go. In those cases, she could indeed stay home without "missing the will of God." In fact, if either of the scenarios I just mentioned were true, then it probably would be better for her to stay home. But even if she does not make the best decision, or even if she makes a wrong decision, God's sovereign plan will go on undaunted. And if she loves God, as Romans 8:28 says, all this will end up working together for her good!

To summarize, God's sovereign will is not the issue in our decision-making process (except that we must be willing to accept what he has ordained), but the moral will, found in the Scriptures, is the most important part. If we want to know what God "wills" for our decisions, we should search the Word of God. And if the Bible does not speak directly to an issue we face, there are principles within it that are sufficient to help us make a good decision. But we must be careful not to look for more guidance or "leading" than God has provided in his Word, or we will end up depending on subjective sources of revelation, like the ones discussed in the next few chapters.

DISCUSSION QUESTIONS

1. Are you glad to know that God has a sovereign will for your life? Why or why not?

2. In what sense can we "find out" the will of God before we make a decision? In what sense can we not?

3. Memorize Deuteronomy 29:29, and explain what the verse means.

4. Discuss this scenario: A man says, "I have become convinced that it was not God's will for me to marry my wife. And because it is not God's will for us to be married, we might as well just give up and get a divorce."

5. How would you answer someone who asked, "How can I find the will of God for my life?"

FEELINGS AND IMPRESSIONS

Many Christians seek for God to guide them, or reveal his will to them, in ways other than through the Scriptures. And when they do, an interesting phenomenon occurs: "non-charismatics" end up acting just like those who believe in continuing revelation. John MacArthur explains this idea further in his book *Reckless Faith:*

> Even people who believe prophecy and divine revelation have ceased sometimes fall into the trap of thinking God speaks directly to us through subjective means. You have undoubtedly heard people say things like, "God is calling me to the mission field," or "God led me to attend this college," or "We feel God wants us to get married." (Perhaps you have even said such things yourself.) Christians who use expressions like these often mean they have had an impression or a strong feeling

that they interpret as a disclosure of the divine will.

Normally people who make such claims have no intention of equating their mental impressions with divine revelation. They regard the subjective "leading of the Lord" as something far less than prophetic. Yet they believe God somehow communicates His will personally to individuals through inner promptings, signs, feelings of peace or uneasiness, strong impressions on the mind, or other similar means. . . .

And the truth is that treating subjective impressions as messages from the Holy Spirit is not really much different from claiming to receive divine revelation. Though most Christians who follow subjective impressions would not dream of listening to extrabiblical "prophecies," in effect they are doing the same thing.[1]

If those who believe in new revelation are right, then we should all be listening for God to speak to us through those subjective means. But if the Bible contains God's complete revelation to us, as I argued in chapter 2, then we should be careful not to practice an approach to decision making that is based on faulty theology. As MacArthur suggests, however, many Christians do just that. And for some examples of how they do it, consider the next group of answers from the missions team headed to Russia. Each one reveals another misunderstood or misapplied idea.

- "God gave me a peace about going, so I know it is right." (feelings)
- "God impressed it upon my heart, prompting me in that direction. In fact, I have developed so much of a burden that I could never stay home." (impressions and promptings)
- "The Lord opened all the doors, so I knew he wanted me to go." (circumstances)
- "I looked for the Lord to speak through my Bible study leader, and he told me that I should go." (counsel)
- "I want to go, and I would not have that desire in my heart unless I am supposed to go." (desires)
- "I prayed about it. And when I pray, I don't only talk to God, but I listen to him. And through prayer he told me to go." (prayer)

Those seven answers contain examples of more misunderstood or misapplied ideas that we will discuss in the next few chapters. This chapter covers only the first two, but I wanted to mention them all here, because they all have a couple of things in common. There are two basic problems with the way many people approach these issues in decision making, and these two problems apply to all the answers given above.

The first problem with feelings, impressions, circumstances, counsel, desires, and prayer is that they are often given *authority* in the decision-making process. None of those issues are unimportant in our choices (nor are they wrong in themselves), but they should never be given authority in our minds. All of these elements, because they are largely subjective, must be submitted to the more objective truth of Scripture, and to the wisdom that comes from the Word. One or more of these considerations may point in a particular direction, but if biblical precept or principle points the other way, then we cannot follow the subjective "signs." The Word must be the ultimate authority in our choices.

But you may be thinking, "Doesn't Scripture talk about all these issues, even in regard to decision making?" Yes, I believe it does. That's why I am not saying that they play no part in God's guidance. They do play an important role many times, but they simply should never have supreme authority in determining our choices. Put another way, you should never make decisions by feelings alone, by impressions alone, by circumstances alone, etc.

The second error we can fall into regarding these matters is the one I have already mentioned: expecting special revelation through the means of feelings, impressions, circumstances, etc. This dovetails with what we learned about God's will in chapter 4. When people say, "I want to know God's will" regarding a choice that Scripture does not address, they are often expecting God to reveal some specific information that is not in the Word. And it is through these various phenomena that they expect to hear from God. You can see this error reflected in the wording of some of the team's answers: "I knew he wanted me to go," "I looked for the Lord to speak through my Bible study leader," and "through prayer God told me to go."

This is why I think it is true that many Christians, who would say that they do not believe in new revelation, are essentially seeking new revelation in their decision making. They may have a theology of "cessationism" in their view of revelation, but in their everyday practice they contradict that theology by trying to hear God say something that is not in the Bible.[2] And I would suggest that their theology is right, so they should let it shape their practical living. God is speaking today, but he is speaking through his Word alone. So we should not say "God told me," "God revealed to me," or any similar language unless we are referring to something we have learned or remembered from our study of the Scriptures.[3]

So with those ideas in mind—that you should not give authority to these phenomena, and that you should not view them as a means of special revelation—we can begin to discuss each one individually, with the goal of learning about the dangers they can present.

THE ROLE OF FEELINGS

When you approach a decision, or even after you have made one, you may experience various feelings such as un-easiness, happiness, contentment, exhilaration, butterflies in your stomach, and so on. Such feelings are important, but their role is often misunderstood, and they are all too often given authority in our choices. But you should never make a decision, stick with one, or abandon one, depending on how you feel about it. This is contrary to the worldly advice that says, "Just follow your heart." When people say that, they mean you should let your feelings or emotions guide you, but that is far from what the Bible says. Proverbs 28:26, for instance, says, "He who trusts in his own heart is a fool" (cf. Jer. 17:9). And the biblical term "heart" does not actually even refer to our emotions. It is a word that speaks primarily of our rational and volitional faculties (cf. Gen. 6:5; Prov. 23:7, Mark 7:21).

Decisions based on emotion are often unwise, because our feelings can mislead us. You could feel great about something and it could be totally wrong, and you could feel terrible about something and it could be totally right. So we need to examine our subjective feelings based on the objective truth of the Word of God. For example, consider a very common way in which Christians talk. We say: "I have a peace about it" or "I just don't have a peace about it." One missions team member said it this way: "God gave me a peace about going, so I knew it was right." When Christians say this, they are usually referring to a positive or negative emotion they are experiencing.[4] And though I am reluctant to criticize an idea that most Christians hold dear, there are some big problems with that kind of thinking.

One problem is that the Bible does not use the word "peace" in the way we are using it. The term never clearly refers to an emotion or feeling. The closest possibility is Philippians 4:7, which says "the peace of God, which surpasses all comprehension, shall guard your hearts and minds in Christ Jesus." But it is difficult to conceive of how a feeling can "guard your hearts and minds," so it seems better to understand the term "peace" in the way it is almost always used in the Bible—the absence of conflict (in this case, between man and God).[5] If the word does have any reference to feelings, then based on the verse before it we would have to say it refers to the *absence* of a certain feeling, namely anxiety (see Phil. 4:6). But I would suggest that the common idea that this verse is referring to a "feeling of peace" has been read into it from our experience. It is much more likely that Paul is saying that when we are anxious and we pray, we can remember that God has reconciled us to himself through the cross, and that since he is our friend, we have nothing to worry about. In other words, the ultimate answer for anxiety is "the gospel of peace" (Eph. 6:15).[6]

Another problem with making choices based on whether we "have a peace about it" is that emotions are simply not good indicators of the rightness or wisdom of a decision. So you could feel "at peace" about something that is wrong or unwise. For instance, I have heard Christians claim to have an inner peace when they were clearly and obviously disobeying God, even while they were pursuing an adulterous relationship. And here is a biblical example of this kind of self-deception:

If ever anyone was out of God's will, it was Jonah. God commanded Jonah to go to Ninevah, which was to the north and to the east. But Jonah, the reluctant prophet, immediately headed to the south and to the west, and boarded a ship sailing out into the Mediterranean. After the boat put out to sea, a tremendous storm arose, and the pagan sailors were terrified.

But Jonah didn't worry—he was asleep in the lower deck of the boat. He had peace, perfect peace, in the midst of the storm. Yet the prophet was completely out of the will of God.[7]

You could also have a lack of "peace" when a particular decision is right. Our Lord Jesus, for example, certainly did not have good feelings in the garden of Gethsemane when he was considering his decision to accept God's plan for the cross. The Bible says he was "deeply grieved, to the point of death" (Matt. 26:38). He was "in agony," and as he was praying "His sweat became like drops of blood, falling down upon the ground" (Luke 22:44). Our Lord and Savior could have said, "I cannot do this because I do not have a peace about it," but thank God he did not base his decision on his feelings! Imagine if we would cancel every wedding where the groom or bride had nervous feelings beforehand—very few people would be married! And we often get "butterflies" or more serious feelings of anxiety when we need to confront someone, or when we get an opportunity to share the gospel with an unbeliever. Should we not do these good things just because we feel bad about them?

There may be significant reasons why you have bad feelings about a particular choice (such as a troubled conscience), but that alone should not determine how you choose. You would have to examine those feelings, through the Word and the counsel of others, and try to understand why you are feeling them. Then you should respond to those emotions in a biblical manner. The following paragraphs from Garry Friesen are helpful for putting our feelings in the right perspective:

> There are two things we must bear in mind about our emotions. The first is that they can be greatly influenced by a host of things: our health, our upbringing, fatigue, medication, the weather, our diet, our hormonal balance, a news report, the feelings of others—in sum, everything that influences our immediate perception of reality.
>
> The second factor is that emotions can affect our lives in one of two ways. They can function either as initiators or as responders. They can be the means whereby one determines "reality," or they can be the means whereby one responds to truth. When a person makes decisions on the basis of objective truth, he is on solid ground, and his emotions find their proper place in expressing his response to reality. . . .

Furthermore, the believer who evaluates his walk with the Lord primarily on the basis of subjective feelings is vulnerable to "spiritual seasickness"— the cumulative effect of being "like the surf of the sea driven and tossed by the wind" (James 1:6). Such an individual may experience euphoric "highs" and despondent "lows" with neither extreme being directly related to God's work in his life.[8]

So be careful not to give too much authority to your feelings, in your decision making, or in any other area of your life. Instead, anchor yourself to God's eternal Word, and you will not be tossed around by the storms that hit you. As the hymn writer says, "How firm a foundation, ye saints of the Lord, is laid for your faith in his excellent Word."

THE ROLE OF IMPRESSIONS, PROMPTINGS, AND "BURDENS"

The next team member mentioned all three of these ideas in her answer: "God impressed it upon my heart, prompting me in that direction. In fact, I have developed so much of a burden that I could never stay home." It is not unusual to hear Christians use those kinds of words frequently in the context of decision making. And when they do, they are usually describing a phenomenon in which a thought pops into their heads (perhaps repeatedly), or when they have some other kind of strong impression in their minds and hearts that they should do something.

Many people erroneously think that God speaks to us, or reveals his will to us, through what they call "impressions," "promptings," "burdens," or "the still small voice of God." The biggest problem with such an approach to guidance is that God does not speak in any way other than through his Word, as we have discussed. But it is also fascinating to see how expressions that are not even biblical can become an integral part of the vocabulary of Christian culture. No doubt, it would surprise some to learn that none of those terms I just mentioned are even used that way in Scripture. You can comb your concordance for the words impression, prompting, and burden, and you will never find them used in the context of God's guidance or decision making!

As for "the still small voice of God," that expression comes from a King James Version mistranslation of 1 Kings 19:12, where God appears to Elijah *after* "the sound of a gentle blowing" (a correct translation). In the story, that soft wind was merely a providential event designed to get Elijah's attention; it was not the source of revelation or guidance. The "word from God" came to Elijah after he heard the sound, when God spoke to him verbally (vv. 13–18). But despite the lack of biblical evidence for this kind of "leading of the Lord," Christians continue to insist that they "hear his voice" in such ways. One well-known pastor distributes an outline called "How to Hear the Voice of God," which contains this advice:

There is perhaps nothing more wonderful or more necessary than for a child of His to learn to hear the voice of God . . . to know His will and how to do it.

Some small-souled critics mock this quest, supposing it is either a vain pursuit of mysticism or an "umbilical" practice divorced from the Scriptures. But it is neither.[9]

This pastor then states categorically that "the Bible is clear in demonstrating this possibility," but does not offer any biblical evidence to support his claim. He then cites the experience of "most of the greatest Christians in history," saying that they "often record their hearing God's voice," and quotes "one of the most beloved songs in recent history" as further support ("And he walks with me, and he talks with me . . ."). Finally, his instructions about "how to hear the voice of God" culminate with this advice:

While alone and quiet, listen with your heart. Don't strain your ears for an audible sound. The Bible describes this order of the Lord's communication with us as a "still small voice." Further, expect His voice to come more *by impressions*, that is, by *thoughts or ideas* which begin to form as you are quiet and worshipful in His presence." [emphasis his][10]

I do not want to disparage this pastor's commendable desire to hear from God and learn his will, nor do I want to belittle the experience of "most of the greatest Christians in history." And I certainly do not want to be the villain who ruins your enjoyment when singing "In the Garden"! But I do want to suggest that this approach to "hearing from God," because it is not based on a sound interpretation of Scripture, arises more from our natural thinking and experience than it does from the Holy Spirit. It is understandable that so many Christians would take this approach (by default), because it is the way we naturally view these things, until our thinking is modified by a further study of the Word. And if I am right, that it is human nature to mistake impressions for divine guidance, then we would expect false religions invented by man to include the same kind of thinking. And they do. For example, consider the most important Mormon "evangelism verse":

> And when ye shall receive these things, I would exhort you that ye would ask God, the Eternal Father, in the name of Christ, if these things are not true; and if ye shall ask with a sincere heart, with real intent, having faith in Christ, he will manifest the truth of it unto you, by the power of the Holy Ghost. (Moroni 10:4)

I have talked to dozens of Mormons who have told me that they were converted to their religion by a strong impression in their hearts which told them it was true (following the advice of that verse). They say this profound experience they had could not be explained in any other way than the leading of God himself. So in effect, they based the most important decision of their lives on a subjective source of guidance. But as I have told them repeatedly, this experience they have had has no more validity in determining truth than did Hitler's sincere belief that God had called him to exterminate the "inferior races." One can be utterly sincere, and still be sincerely wrong. I do not deny that such people have had some kind of experience, but personal experience is not the source of truth, no matter how amazing or profound it may be. Again, Garry Friesen's thoughts on this topic are helpful:

> How can I tell whether these impressions are from God or from some other source? This is a critical question. For impressions could be produced by any number of sources: God, Satan, an angel, a demon, human emotions (such as fear or ecstasy), hormonal imbalance, insomnia, medication, or an upset stomach. Sinful impressions (temptations) may be exposed for what they are by the Spirit-sensitized conscience and the Word of God. But beyond that, one encounters a subjective quagmire of uncertainty. For in nonmoral areas, Scripture gives no guidelines for distinguishing the voice of the Spirit from the voice of the self—or any other potential "voice." And experience offers no reliable means of identification either (which is why the question

comes up in the first place). . . . Tremendous frustration has been experienced by sincere Christians who have earnestly but fruitlessly sought to decipher the code of the inward witness.[11]

While I was doing the initial research for this part of the book, I took a break one day to get some lunch at a Chinese restaurant. Would you believe what I found when I opened my fortune cookie that day? It said, "Following inner promptings brings quiet accomplishment (Peking Noodle Company)!" So let me ask you: Is your decision-making method more like biblical Christianity, or more like Mormonism and Buddhism? If you are listening for God to speak in some way other than Scripture, or if you are allowing feelings and impressions to have authority in your choices, then I would suggest you need a Copernican revolution in your thinking. Let God's Word become the center of your decision-making process.

THE LEADING OF THE LORD

At this point someone might say, "You've been saying that God does not speak in this way, but what about his leading and guiding? Doesn't he sometimes use impressions, thoughts, etc. to guide us?" I believe the answer lies in the distinctions discussed in the last chapter between the sovereign will of God and the revealed will of God. He does use impressions to guide us in the sovereign sense of guidance, accomplishing his foreordained plan down to the smallest detail, but remember that plan includes even the bad impressions and thoughts that come into our minds. God does not plant them in our minds, as James 1:13 makes clear, but he does allow them for some reason.

But when it comes to the kind of guidance we are seeking in order to make a good decision, the only role that impressions should play is that we should evaluate them based on Scripture and wisdom, to see if they might make some contribution to our decision-making process. Such thoughts or impressions are not "God speaking to me," so they may or may not make a contribution depending on what God has already said in his Word. For example, suppose you begin to get a strong impression or repeated thought in your mind that says, "Give money to the church." If you are not doing that already, then you need to start doing it—not because that thought came to your mind, but because it is in Scripture (1 Cor. 16:1–2). However, if a similar impression hits you, "Give $300 per month to the church," you should take some time to evaluate that idea, because it may or may not be wise. If it is, then do it (but not because "God told me to"). And if you are watching some televangelist who parades orphans in front of the screen and asks you for a faith promise of $10,000 you do not have, and which would place you in debt, do not do it! No matter how much you feel obligated to do it, no matter how strong of a burden is pressing upon your heart, you should reject that idea because it is not the wisest or most scriptural way to use your resources (Rom. 13:8; Eccl. 5:4–5).

Finally, "the leading of the Spirit" is often mentioned in regard to both feelings and impressions. Christians say things like "I feel led" to do this or that,[12] or "the Spirit led me." Frequently when people use such terminology, they are not referring to the Holy Spirit's work of helping us to understand and obey God's Word, which is the way the Bible uses it (Rom. 8:14; Gal. 5:18). Rather they are referring primarily to the Spirit leading us to make particular decisions through inner promptings. And this is what some teachers mean when they talk about "the subjective leading of the Spirit." Personally, I think that terminology is misleading, because it can promote the assumption that our inner impulses are revelations from the Spirit and therefore should be given authority.[13] For that reason I prefer not to use that terminology in the context of decision making. But if it is so ingrained in Christian language that we have to continue saying it, then I would challenge you to use it with the right ideas in mind. Think about how the Spirit does lead, according to the Scriptures, and remember that he does not do so through cryptic impressions.

John MacArthur has some more good thoughts on this topic, which provide for us a fitting conclusion:

> Scripture never commands us to tune into any inner voice. We're commanded to study and meditate on Scripture (Josh. 1:8; Ps. 1:1–2). We're instructed to cultivate wisdom and discernment (Prov. 4:5–8). We're told to walk wisely and make the most of our

time (Eph. 5:15–16). We're ordered to be obedient to God's commands (Deut. 28:1–2; John 15:14). But we are never encouraged to listen for inner promptings.

On the contrary, we are warned that our hearts are so deceitful and desperately wicked that we cannot understand them (Jer. 17:9). Surely this should make us very reluctant to heed promptings and messages that arise from within ourselves.[14]

DISCUSSION QUESTIONS

1. Discuss this line from an old song by a "Christian" singer: "It can't be wrong, when it feels so right."
2. How often do you think Christians make decisions based on their feelings? Why do you think that is?
3. Does the Philippians 4:7 discussion on pages 66–67 cause you to look at that verse in a different way? If so, how?
4. Discuss these words from the famous hymn, "In the Garden": "And he walks with me, and he talks with me, and he tells me I am his own."
5. How does the Holy Spirit lead us? How does he *not* lead us?

SIX

CIRCUMSTANCES, COUNSEL, DESIRES, AND PRAYER

In the last chapter we learned about some mistakes that Christians should avoid regarding feelings and impressions. They should never be given absolute authority (or viewed as the "bottom line" in our choices) and they should not be viewed as a source of divine revelation (as if God "speaks" to us through them). Those warnings also apply to the phenomena we will be discussing in this chapter. Circumstances, counsel, desires, and prayer are also issues that are often misunderstood or misapplied by Christians in our decision making. This chapter will not contain an exhaustive discussion of those issues, but hopefully it will make you aware of the biggest dangers regarding each of them.

THE ROLE OF CIRCUMSTANCES

Situations we find ourselves in, events that transpire around us in our lives—these are important factors in deci-

sion making. However, they are *not* "road signs on the high-
way of life, put there by God to reveal his will to us, or to
tell us which way to go." Such an understanding is a misunderstanding. Circumstances are not to be given authority in our decisions, and they are not to be viewed as God
speaking to us. Haddon Robinson explains why in a section
entitled "Circumstantial Evidence":

> Many people overemphasize the importance of cir-
> cumstances in the decision-making process. Al-
> though circumstances are a factor in nearly all
> decisions, it is important that we not let circum-
> stances dictate the decisions we make.
>
> Many people consider circumstances to be
> God's voice—they depend on circumstantial evi-
> dence. But circumstances are simply the factors that
> bring us to the point of decision. They often outline
> the decision that must be made, but circumstances
> in themselves are not necessarily signs of God's
> guidance.
>
> I'm reminded of the Rorshach Test, the psycho-
> logical test featuring the big ink blots. Psychologists
> ask their clients to describe what they see in the
> blots. One person sees a beautiful butterfly. Another
> sees, in the same blots, demons coming to claim his
> soul. Circumstances often work the same way. The
> things we see in them often say more about us than
> they do about what is really happening.

Circumstances don't provide us with the guidance we need to make good decisions. If we try to
figure out what God is doing in our circumstances,
we will often come away more confused than informed. We see this truth in a humorous incident
recorded in the final chapter in the Book of Acts.

Paul and his physician friend, Luke, were ship-
wrecked and washed ashore on the island of Malta.
In order to keep warm, Paul gathered some sticks.
As he put the bundle on the fire, a viper sank its
fangs into the flesh of his hand. When the people
of Malta saw what happened, they interpreted the
circumstance in light of God's providence: "This
man must be a murderer; for though he escaped
from the sea, Justice has not allowed him to live"
(Acts 28:4).

But Paul shook off the viper into the fire, and its
poison apparently had no effect. When the people
saw this new set of circumstances, they completely
reversed themselves. Acts tells us, "They changed
their minds and said he was a god" (28:6).

In both cases, these people were doing their very
best to read the circumstances. And in both cases,
they were wrong![1]

One way that Christians often refer to circumstances in
decision making that can be problematic is the idea of
"open and closed doors." One of the members of our fic-

tional missions team, mentioned in the last chapter, said that he decided to go because "God has opened all the doors, so I know he wants me to go." The problems with that statement are the ones we have been discussing: he has given undue authority to circumstances, and he has assumed that they are a revelation of the divine will. But he also needs to realize that all the doors could be open and it still could be a wrong or unwise choice. And you need to realize this, too, if you want to make good decisions: Just because a door is open does not mean that you should walk through it!

In the New Testament, the phrase "open door" is used five times, and each time it refers to an opportunity, particularly an opportunity for ministry. If you look at those uses of the phrase, you will notice that although the apostles may have had an open door, they did not always enter it. One example is what Paul says in 2 Corinthians 2:12–13:

> Now when I came to Troas for the gospel of Christ and when a door was opened for me in the Lord, I had no rest for my spirit, not finding Titus my brother; but taking my leave of them, I went on to Macedonia.

The Old Testament also contains an interesting example of an open door of opportunity that was not entered. In 1 Samuel 24, David was fleeing from Saul and Saul's band of 3,000 men. David and his men were hiding in a cave, and Saul left his own men to go alone into that same cave to "cover his feet" (a Hebrew phrase for "using the facilities"). David's men told him, "God is delivering your enemy into your hand! Kill him!" But David did not read this opportunity as direction from the Lord, because it would have been contrary to what God had already revealed. David told his men, "Far be it from me because of the Lord that I should do this thing to my lord, the Lord's anointed, to stretch out my hand against him, since he is the Lord's anointed" (1 Sam. 24:6).

Be careful to recognize that "open doors" and "closed doors" are not revelations from God as to what choice you should make. They are important factors that must be evaluated according to the Word and godly wisdom, but they should never settle the issue by themselves. Also, be careful not to fall into the trap of thinking that circumstances confirm or deny the legitimacy of a decision after you have made it. An example would be what a friend once told me about his choice to attend seminary and prepare for pastoral ministry. He had been offered money from some family members to cover the costs, but he decided not to take it, because he said that he wanted God to "confirm" his choice by providing a good job for him somewhere near the school. He felt that if he got a good job, this meant that it was God's will for him to study for the ministry. I cautioned him about this, however, mentioning that whether God provided a job or not did not necessarily mean anything. He might get a great job even if it was wrong or unwise for him to be in seminary. On the other hand he could hit a brick wall trying to find a job, but it still might be a good choice to attend, especially if someone were willing to pay his way!

He did get a good job, by the way, and did make it through seminary without the help of others. And that raises the questions, "Didn't God plan that? And doesn't God control all the events in our lives?" Yes, he does, and his sovereign control of all things for the good of his people is called his providence.

THE HAND OF PROVIDENCE

The Westminster Confession defines God's providence in this way:

> God the great Creator of all things doth uphold, direct, dispose, and govern all creatures, actions, and things, from the greatest even to the least, by his most wise and holy providence, according to his infallible foreknowledge, and the free and immutable counsel of his own will, to the praise of the glory of his wisdom, power, justice, goodness, and mercy. (V, 1)

God's providence is a great blessing, for which we should thank him continually. But as we discussed in chapter 4 regarding the sovereign will of God, we cannot "read" his providence or discover what he has planned ahead of time. And we should not attempt to do so. His providential plan is a part of the "secret things" that belong to him alone. We must focus on what he has revealed in his Word, as Deuteronomy 29:29 says.

Proverbs 20:24 makes the same point when it says, "Man's steps are ordained by the Lord, how then can man understand his way?" Because the Lord works in mysterious ways, it is extremely difficult to "read" his providence with any degree of accuracy. As Garry Friesen writes,

> The only time that circumstances can be "read" is when a divine interpretation is placed upon them by supernatural revelation. Apart from such revelation, circumstances may be taken to mean almost anything. Just listen to this imaginary but believable discussion concerning the "message" God was trying to convey when lightning struck a church steeple.
>
> "God is telling us to relocate in the suburbs."
>
> "Oh no, I think it's quite obvious He's saying 'no' to our expansion plans."
>
> "Maybe the Lord is telling us that there is sin holding back the work in our church."[2]

This is how "non-charismatics," even though they believe that supernatural signs have ceased as a means of revelation, are still (in their practical living) looking for supernatural signs as a means of revelation! They view particular occurrences as "signs" that God wants them to do this or that. Some even use that word: "I took it as a sign from God when . . ."

But as we said about the sovereign will of God, his providence plays basically no part in our decision-making process, except that we need to be willing to accept whatever happens as a part of God's plan. Paul Helm captures this idea well in his book *The Providence of God:*

> How does divine providence guide? How can divine providence guide? As we have seen, there is a sense in which, since all that happens is under the control of God, all that happens is under his guidance. Nevertheless, the fact that everything that happens is subject to divine providence . . . in and of itself offers no guidance as to what you or I ought to do. The events of our lives tell us what is and has been; by themselves they do not indicate what ought to be. For what is and has been includes not only all the goodness and kindness that there has ever been, but all the viciousness and depravity as well.
>
> What is needed to show us what ought to be the case is some ethical standard or standards, some measure of rightness and wrongness. Christians believe that there is such a standard to be found in the *command* of God. It is crucially important, therefore, when considering the matter of divine provi-

dence and divine guidance, to distinguish between the will of God as meaning *what happens*, and the will of God as meaning *what ought to happen*.[3]

That second aspect of the will of God—what he says ought to happen in his Word—is what you should be concerned about when you face a decision. But to say that the providence of God plays basically no part in our decision-making process is not to say that God does not exercise his providence in connection with our choices. Although the providence of God is not revelatory in itself, it is the "vehicle" in which he brings his revelation to us. Perhaps this will help those who have experienced apparent "signs" to put such experiences in a proper biblical perspective: God speaks to us through the Word and the Word alone, but he does use circumstances to bring the Word to us, or to bring us to the Word.

As an example, imagine that you go to church one Sunday, and during the discussion time in your Sunday school class, someone at your table mentions that he has been struggling with the sin of jealousy toward a co-worker. This hits you right between the eyes, because at that moment you realize that you have had the same kind of thoughts and feelings toward one of your co-workers. You realize that this is a violation of numerous commands in Scripture, and that you need to confess this to God and change in that area of your life. God has spoken to you in that situation, but he has spoken to you through his Word (the tenth commandment, Ps. 73, etc.). He has not spoken to you through the circumstance itself, even though it was an amazing co-incidence. His providence in the circumstance was merely the vehicle through which his Word came to you (and God does do that sort of thing often).

You might think that the distinction I have made above is an acute case of hairsplitting, but it really does have prac-tical implications. If you have the wrong view—that God speaks to you through the events that he sovereignly or-chestrates—then what will you be thinking the next week when you sit down at the same table and the same person says that he has been thinking about moving on to another church? Especially if you have been having similar thoughts yourself, you will be likely to view this event as another "word from the Lord." But unless some principle in the Scriptures would lead you out of that church, it may not be the right or wise thing to do.

So even the most amazing coincidence is not a "sign" of God's leading, but we can always thank God for the way in which he "causes all things to work together for good" (Rom. 8:28).

THE ROLE OF COUNSEL

When it comes to advice we receive from others about our choices, two extremes must be avoided. One extreme is seeking too little counsel from others. These verses from Proverbs should be sufficient to warn us of that danger:

The way of a fool is right in his own eyes, but a wise man is he who listens to counsel. (12:15)

Through presumption comes nothing but strife, but with those who receive counsel is wisdom. (13:10)

Without consultation, plans are frustrated, but with many counselors they succeed. (15:22)

On the other hand, consider the benefits of wise counsel mentioned in some other Proverbs:

Listen to counsel and accept discipline, that you may be wise the rest of your days. (19:20)

Prepare plans by consultation, and make war by wise guidance. (20:18)

Oil and perfume make the heart glad, so a man's counsel is sweet to his friend. (27:9)

So beware of making decisions (especially big ones) without seeking and receiving input from others. But there is another extreme you must avoid, and that is expecting too much from counsel. We also learn from the book of Proverbs, and from the book of Job, that even well-intentioned advisors can be anything from inadequate to embarrassingly wrong. So it is irresponsible for us to allow someone else to make our decisions for us, or to look for God to speak through someone's counsel. In fact, the only time God speaks through other people is when they are speaking his Word.

Other than that, their words are merely advice that we need to evaluate carefully in light of Scripture.

The mistake of overestimating counsel is illustrated by another of the missions team members. When asked why he decided to go on the trip, he said, "I looked for the Lord to speak through my Bible study leader, and he told me I should go." That was irresponsible on his part, an easy way out of the hard work of good decision making. But it also may have been irresponsible on the part of the Bible study leader, if he did not make clear that he was providing a suggestion and not a "word from the Lord." We should tell anyone who seeks advice from us, "I am not God! And what he has to say is much more important than what I have to say."

THE ROLE OF DESIRES

There are also two extremes to be avoided regarding our desires. One is the idea that desires are unimportant or even detrimental to God's guidance in our lives. Some people think that the last thing God would want them to do is what they want to do. They think any enjoyment in their lives is a lack of self-denial, or merely "of the flesh." So if they take great pleasure in working outdoors doing physical labor, they get a job as an accountant. They love the fine arts, so they drive a garbage truck, thinking that it somehow pleases God to deny their desires. Some Christians have even gone to the mission field because they didn't want to live overseas, so they figured God must have been calling them there!

That is not biblical thinking. As we will discuss at length in a later chapter, God works in and through our desires, and he even guides us in some situations through them. But the other extreme is to give our desires too much authority—to follow them when other, more important considerations should have more weight.

I have heard people say, "Love God and do what you want." There is some truth in that statement, because God does often lead us through our desires when we are loving and following him. But it is also possible for us to genuinely love God, but still not have the best desires in a particular situation. None of us loves God with all our heart, soul, mind, and strength at all times—nor do we even come close. So our desires may be wrong, and even when they are right, it may not be the wisest choice to follow them.

Others have said that if you are the right kind of person (saved, sanctified, serving, etc.), then what you want to do will be what God wants you to do. Again, there is some truth in that statement, because in some cases what we desire is indeed the best way for us to go. But unfortunately that approach omits the all-important concept of wisdom. There are times in the lives of even the most devout Christians when what we desire is not the wisest move. So wisdom must be given more authority than our desires, if we are to be biblical in our decision making.

So you need to examine your desires based on Scripture,

and go against them if the Word points you another way. And even in issues outside the direct purview of the Bible, you should first ask the question, "What is the wisest choice?" Sometimes what you want will not be the wisest way to go.

Hopefully you can see what is wrong with the statement made by the missions team member who said, "I want to go, and I wouldn't have that desire in my heart unless I am supposed to go." Not necessarily. It might be a wrong desire, or it might be a good desire that is outweighed by scriptural principles or sound wisdom.

THE ROLE OF PRAYER

Prayer is of the utmost importance in biblical decision making, but its role is often misunderstood or misapplied. The last missions team member said, "I prayed about it. And when I pray, I don't just talk to God but he talks to me. And through prayer he told me to go." There are several problems with that approach. First and most obvious, she believes that she has received special revelation, either through audible words or a "still small voice" in the form of feelings or impressions. And as we learned in the previous chapter, the Bible teaches that God does not speak in that manner.

But there is also no biblical command to "listen to God" in prayer. In fact, the words for prayer in Scripture, by definition, refer to communicating our thoughts, feelings, and requests to God, and they contain no idea of him communicating to us. In other words, when we "pray," we are the only ones praying. The terms for prayer in Scripture (Heb. *pahlal, tephillah*; Greek *proseuche*) are never used of God.[4] We talk to God through prayer; he talks to us through his Word. So the idea of "listening to God in prayer" reflects a misunderstanding. And so do the words of one Christian song:

> *In stillness and simplicity, I hear the Spirit silently . . .*
> *Is the reason we're not still*
> *To hear him speak,*
> *Because we don't believe he will?*[5]

Following the advice in that song, I used to sit quietly for hours, waiting to hear something from God. Sometimes a thought would enter my mind that I was convinced was from God, and I would then act on it as soon as possible. But as time went on, I began to notice that the thoughts I "received" sometimes led me into trouble. They were not always the wisest choices to make. I remember that sometimes other Christians warned me about the plans I made because of these "quiet times," but I would not listen to them, of course. I had heard from God, so I barreled ahead every time. But as I said, I began to notice that sometimes my friends ended up being right, and the ideas "God gave me" were not such great ideas after all. So I was in a dilemma: either I had to blame God for leading me the wrong way, or I had to rearrange my thinking about God's leading.

I do believe that we should take time to be quiet, and to meditate on the principles of Scripture and how they can apply to our lives. And a good time to do this is while we are praying to the Lord in a "quiet time." But we should be praying for a greater understanding of Scripture (Ps. 25:4) and more wisdom in applying it (James 1:5), not for God to speak to us in some extrabiblical fashion. God will not tell you, "Go on a missions trip," either audibly or through some inner voice. But in his providence he will bring to mind principles from Scripture that apply to your choices, if you have been faithful to study diligently "as a workman who does not need to be ashamed, handling accurately the word of truth" (2 Tim. 2:15). Do not view prayer as an "easy way out," by thinking that prayer alone will help you make good decisions. You need to think carefully and biblically about your choices if you want to make good ones.

That last thought leads to a good conclusion for this part on "How *Not* to Make Decisions." I have said over and over again, in different ways, that making good decisions is a matter of using our *minds* to apply the objective truth of Scripture. Your choices should be based on sound wisdom rather than subjective considerations that are primarily within yourself. All of the errors we have discussed are lacking that sound wisdom in some way, and they are summarized and illustrated well in a conversation that took place on Christian television between a talk show host and a famous "faith healer." The host asked the healer how to receive the guidance of God for our decisions, and the healer replied that God leads us primarily in these four ways:

1. Visions and dreams
2. Prophecies
3. Internal impressions
4. Circumstances

When asked how to discern when God is speaking to us, this man said, "You know when you know that you know." He then elaborated: "The way you know something is not from God is when it's from your mind. God doesn't speak to our minds, but to our spirits."

That is a veritable primer on how *not* to make decisions![6] If you can see that, and you would like to know how *to* make decisions according to the Scriptures, read on. Perhaps you even feel like this first part of the book has taken away from you most of the ways in which you have made decisions up until now. If that is the case, keep going to the second part, and take heart—God has a more biblical plan, which will serve you much better than your old one!

DISCUSSION QUESTIONS

1. What do you think about this advice: "Pray hard about your choice, and if God opens a door, go for it!"

2. What was God saying to America on September 11, 2001? (Yes, this is a trick question!)

3. What standard should we use to evaluate the advice we get from others? How should we do that?

4. Describe some good desires and some bad desires, according to the Bible. When can a good desire become a bad one?

5. Do you think you have been making some of your decisions in the wrong way? How?

PART TWO

HOW *TO* MAKE DECISIONS

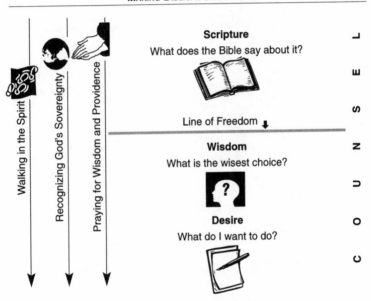

Walking in the Spirit

Recognizing God's Sovereignty

Praying for Wisdom and Providence

Scripture
What does the Bible say about it?

Line of Freedom

Wisdom
What is the wisest choice?

Desire
What do I want to do?

COUNSEL

SEVEN

THE PREREQUISITES FOR BIBLICAL DECISION MAKING

What kind of person do you need to be in order to make good decisions? In the chapter after this one, we will learn about how God leads people, but first we must learn about who he leads. According to the Scriptures, God does not lead everyone. So unless you are the right kind of person during the process of making a decision, you can have no confidence that you will gain the wisdom and guidance necessary to make a good choice. Unless you are the kind of person who is walking in the Spirit, recognizing the sovereignty of God, and praying for wisdom and providence, you will seek in vain for the direction you need and turn down the wrong road time after time.

WALKING IN THE SPIRIT

The Bible often uses the word-picture of "walking" to represent the Christian life as it should be lived (cf. Gal. 5:16;

1 John 1:7, 2:6). The Lord, in his wisdom, chose this picture so that when we think of our "walk" with Christ, we would remember some important truths implied in that word. One such truth is that the Christian life is not one of perfection, but of direction. To be "walking" is to be headed somewhere, not to have arrived (cf. Phil. 3:12–14). Another helpful element of the word-picture is that walking is a process of taking one step at a time, which can begin again as quickly as it ends.

As you face decisions every day, you need to be walking in the Spirit before you can expect him to lead you. This means that you must be confessing your sin and you must have an attitude of willingness to do whatever God wants you to do. But before we discuss more about those matters, we need to consider the fact that no one can be "walking" anywhere unless he or she has taken the first step. And in this case, you cannot be "walking in the Spirit" unless you have first been born again by the Spirit.

Jesus told Nicodemus, "Unless one is born again, he cannot see the kingdom of God" (John 3:3). The unregenerate state of man is one of spiritual blindness; he has no ability to even understand God's truth, let alone be guided by it. Only the person who has been born again by the Spirit of God is able to understand the truth and wisdom God has revealed in his Word. Paul explains this truth thoroughly in 1 Corinthians 2:9–14:

> As it is written, "Things which eye has not seen and
> ear has not heard, and which have not entered the

heart of man, all that God has prepared for those who love Him." For to us God revealed them through the Spirit; for the Spirit searches all things, even the depths of God. For who among men knows the thoughts of a man except the spirit of the man, which is in him? Even so the thoughts of God no one knows except the Spirit of God. Now we have received, not the spirit of the world, but the Spirit who is from God, that we might know the things freely given to us by God. . . . But a natural man does not accept the things of the Spirit of God; for they are foolishness to him, and he cannot understand them, because they are spiritually appraised.

In John 10:27, Jesus spoke of guidance and direction when he said, "My sheep hear My voice, and I know them, and they follow Me." In the verse before he made clear that not everyone belongs to his flock when he told the Pharisees, "You are not of My sheep." The Good Shepherd "leads me beside quiet waters" (Ps. 23:2) only when I am one of his sheep. Romans 8 says, "Those who are in the flesh cannot please God" (v. 7) and "All who are being led by the Spirit of God, these are sons of God" (v. 14).

Are you one of the Lord's sheep? Have you turned from the flesh (your way of living) to the Spirit (God's way of living)? Have you been adopted into his family as a son or daughter through faith in his Son, Jesus Christ? If not, that is the first step you must take if you want to walk in the

Spirit and be led by the Lord. Repent from your sins and trust in Christ alone to save you; then you will be eligible to receive the wisdom and direction of God for your decisions.[1]

If you have taken that "first step," however, you cannot stop there, or you will not be walking in the Spirit, you will just be standing still, going nowhere! You must continue on your journey by repenting from your sins and believing in Christ every day, even every moment. Jesus said, "If anyone wishes to come after Me, let him deny himself, and take up his cross *daily*, and follow Me" (Luke 9:23). Psalm 66:18 says, "If I *regard wickedness* in my heart, The Lord will not hear." The occurrence of sin in our lives is not enough to stifle God's leading, but if we hold on to it, cherish it, and fail to confess and forsake it, we cannot expect to receive his wisdom (cf. James 1:5–7). Proverbs 28:13 says, "He who conceals his transgressions will not prosper, but he who confesses and forsakes them will find compassion."[2]

So to be walking in the Spirit, you must be regularly confessing your sin and turning from it. But you also must be willing to do whatever God wants you to do as you approach your decisions. To put it another way, God's guidance is dependent upon your commitment to obedience. It is hypocrisy to ask God to help you make a decision when you have already decided what you are going to do, regardless of what he says. It is rebellion to say that you will only accept God's leading, if you can approve of the path he has chosen for you.

The story of Paul's conversion in Acts 22:6–10 illustrates this truth. Paul, known then as Saul, had been persecuting Christians as a representative of the Jewish leaders, and was headed to the city of Damascus to pick up some captured believers, whom he would then take back to Jerusalem for imprisonment, torture, execution, or all of the above. On the road to Damascus he was knocked to the ground by a bright light, and he heard the voice of Jesus himself telling him that he had been sadly mistaken regarding which group of people had the truth. As he lay on the ground, realizing his life was about to change dramatically, Paul responded to Christ in a way that set an example for all believers to follow.

He did not say, "Could you turn down the light? It's very uncomfortable," or "You shouldn't be so direct, you're making me feel bad." What he said was, "What shall I do, Lord?" When Paul "saw the light" (the majesty of Christ), his response was an attitude of unconditional surrender to God's will, and that remains the attitude of all who will walk in the light. We must be willing to go wherever he leads us, without any exceptions or reservations. Imagine if Paul, in his moment of truth, had said, "Lord, I'll go anywhere you want me to go, but just don't ask me to go into Damascus." This would have been understandable, because going into Damascus meant sure persecution, and maybe even death for Paul ("Hi guys . . . You know those Christians we've been killing—I'm one of them now!"). But if Paul had put this one understandable limitation on what he would do for Christ, the leading of the Lord would have been short-circuited at the very beginning, because Damascus was the very place God wanted him to go (v. 10).

So to receive direction from the Lord and make good decisions, you must be willing to do anything the Lord wants you to do. Romans 14 says this in another way: you must live life under the lordship of Christ. That passage is about Christian liberty, which is the freedom we have before God to enjoy many things we want to do, even if other Christians may not approve of them, as long as they are not prohibited by God's Word (vv. 2–3). But notice in verses 4–9 that Paul describes those who have this liberty as servants of Jesus Christ, who are fully convinced after careful consideration that what they are doing is right, and whose primary motivation is to honor their Lord and Master in everything they do. So someone who tries to excuse his or her own selfish behavior by saying, "I have Christian liberty!" does not understand the meaning of Romans 14. The only true Christian liberty is that which falls squarely under the lordship of Christ—it is the freedom to do what pleases him.

So to make good decisions, you must be one who has submitted yourself to Jesus Christ as Lord (both initially and continually), and that is basically what it means to be walking in the Spirit. As someone once said, "You can't steer a parked car." And God cannot lead you unless you are moving in the direction of Christlikeness, doing those things that you already know are right to do.

RECOGNIZING GOD'S SOVEREIGNTY

This second prerequisite to making biblical decisions means that as you face each choice in life, you must acknowledge and accept the fact that God is sovereign, or in control, of the options you have, the way you end up going, and the results and ramifications of your decisions. In chapter 4, we discussed this aspect of God's government in the world by referring to it as the sovereign or secret will of God (as opposed to the moral or revealed will). It also has often been called the providence of God. As I said in that earlier discussion, we should not try to make decisions by finding out what God has planned in his sovereign will; rather we should concern ourselves with the revealed will of God in the Scriptures. But although the sovereignty of God has no direct bearing on the *activity* of decision making, our understanding and acceptance of it is essential to our *attitude* in the process of decision making.

You must know that God is in control and you must trust in his providence if you are going to be the kind of person he will lead and guide. Recognizing God's sovereignty will bear wonderful fruit in your life, including the fruits of humility, hope, and joy.

It will make you humble.

James 4:13–16 says,

Come now, you who say, "Today or tomorrow, we shall go to such and such a city, and spend a year there and engage in business and make a profit." Yet you do not know what your life will be like tomorrow. You are just a vapor that appears for a little while and then vanishes away. Instead, you ought to say, "If the Lord wills, we shall live and also do this or that." But as it is, you boast in your arrogance; all such boasting is evil.

As Haddon Robinson says, "You ought to make your plans with *a very strong sense of* 'If,' because you don't know what the next day will hold, not to mention the next year."[3] James reminds us how uncertain life is, and how impotent we are to control what happens to us. Our life is not ultimately in our hands, so we do not even know for sure that we will be alive tomorrow.

> Life is that way. It's fragile; it's fleeting. It's like the mist that settles over the valley in the morning. The sun comes up and by 10:00, the mist is gone. It's like the steam from a kettle—no sooner does it appear but it disappears. It's like breath on a cold winter's day—now you see it; now you don't.
>
> We may not realize it, but last week's business trip may have brought us within a second or two, within a yard or two, of a fatal crash. Even now a virus may be lurking in our body, so small it cannot even be seen by a microscope. But that germ may call us away from our plans, our board meetings, and

our comfortable routines, at any time. Life—James tells us—is that way.

We are arrogant, we are proud, and we are boastful if we convince ourselves that we know what will happen next in life. We may think that we're the master of our fate, the captain of our soul, or that we will carry out our plans. But we may be in for a terrible surprise.[4]

Proverbs 16:9 says, "The mind of man plans his way, but the Lord directs his steps." This does not mean that planning is wrong—the Bible never says that. In fact, planning is an important part of wise decision making. But when you make your plans, your attitude must be one of humility before God, realizing that the outcome of those plans is dependent upon his sovereign will. You need to practice the habit of saying, in your heart and with your lips, "If the Lord wills," or "Lord willing." That is not just a pious platitude; it is terminology used repeatedly in Scripture (Acts 18:21; 1 Cor. 4:19; 16:5–7). And saying it repeatedly will help you to cultivate that "strong sense of 'if' " that will make you humble and enable you to receive the grace you need to make good decisions (cf. James 4:6, 10).

It will make you hopeful.

Trusting in God's sovereignty will keep you from despair when your decisions lead you into trouble, and even when you end up making bad decisions. As you read Romans

8:28–39, notice how this famous passage emphasizes the sovereignty of God over all things and also how this truth provides great hope for God's people:

> And we know that God causes all things to work together for good to those who love God, to those who are called according to His purpose. For whom He foreknew, He also predestined to become conformed to the image of His Son, that He might be the first-born among many brethren; and whom He predestined, these He also called; and whom He called, these He also justified; and whom He justified, these He also glorified. What then shall we say to these things? If God is for us, who is against us? He who did not spare His own Son, but delivered Him up for us all, how will He not also with Him freely give us all things? Who will bring a charge against God's elect? God is the one who justifies; who is the one who condemns? Christ Jesus is He who died, yes, rather who was raised, who is at the right hand of God, who also intercedes for us. Who shall separate us from the love of Christ? Shall tribulation, or distress, or persecution, or famine, or nakedness, or peril, or sword? Just as it is written, "For Thy sake we are being put to death all day long; we were considered as sheep to be slaughtered." But in all these things we overwhelmingly conquer through Him who loved us. For I am con-

vinced that neither death, nor life, nor angels, nor principalities, nor things present, nor things to come, nor powers, nor height, nor depth, nor any other created thing, shall be able to separate us from the love of God, which is in Christ Jesus our Lord.

If you love God and are becoming more like Christ (the purpose for which you were called), then you are one of the people God has chosen for eternal glory before the world began, and in your life now everything that happens is a part of his sovereign plan for you. So even though the train of your life may take some difficult turns and endure some bumpy tracks, it will never be derailed. Regardless of what happens as a result of your decisions, or even how inadequate your decision making is, God is still on his throne and you can have the confidence that he will cause everything (even the bad things) to work together for your good.

From this you can see that God's sovereignty is not an ogrely doctrine designed to instill fear in your heart (if you believe in Christ and follow him). No, if you are his faithful child, this truth is intended to give you hope. Even when you misstep, he is one step ahead of you. Even when you stumble or fall, he will silently carry you. And when others try to bring you down, he will lift you up. This is the aspect of God's guidance or leading that we can call his "sovereign guidance," and it is described in Psalm 23 and the great hymn based on it:

All the way my Savior leads me;
what have I to ask beside?
Can I doubt his tender mercy,
who through life has been my guide?
Heav'nly peace, divinest comfort,
here by faith in him to dwell;
for I know, whate're befall me,
Jesus doeth all things well.

It will make you happy.

Realizing that God is in control of your life is one of the biggest answers to the anxiety and fear that plague so many Christians (especially when they are faced with important decisions). After the apostle Paul delivered the Bible's most frank and thorough explanation of God's sovereignty in Romans, chapters 9–11, he did not crawl into a corner and sink into deep depression, complaining that this doctrine makes us all into "puppets," renders our efforts pointless, and causes division between Christians. No, as Paul reflected on his revelation of the sovereignty of God, he broke into a paeon of joyful praise:

Oh, the depth of the riches both of the wisdom and knowledge of God! How unsearchable are His judgments and unfathomable His ways! For who has known the mind of the Lord, or who became His counselor? Or who has first given to Him that it might be paid back to him again? For from Him and

through Him and to Him are all things. To Him be
the glory forever. Amen.

Why did the truth of God's sovereign control bring so
much joy to Paul? I think it was because he had learned to
practice what I call "the spectator principle." Once we understand that God has a plan for this world and for our individual lives, we can begin to see some of what he is doing
in the world and in our lives. You cannot know God's sovereign will before you make a decision, and even afterwards
you will not be able to understand all of what he has
planned and why, but sometimes (many times even, if you
look hard) you will be able to see what he is doing and some
of the reasons why he is doing it. And nothing can bring
more holy delight than watching the Master Artist weave
the tapestry of history, observing the Conductor of the universe orchestrate all things together for our good, and discovering the perfect storyline that has been plotted by the
Divine Director for his own glory.

One example from my own life will serve to illustrate
this truth: Several years ago, my father was diagnosed with
lung cancer and given six months to live. On the day that
he called me from the other side of the country and told
me, I purchased a plane ticket for a flight leaving in two
weeks. I began praying and planning for the week I would
spend with him, as it might be our last together. I then
talked to him every day on the phone about the Lord, looking forward to studying the Bible together with him during

that week. Two days before my flight, however, he passed away unexpectedly. At first I was angry at God that he did not let me see my father before he died, but my wife reminded me gently and lovingly that the Lord knows better than we do and undoubtedly had his reasons for this. By God's grace, I was able to turn from my anger, trust in the Lord, and even pray that he might show me some of the reasons why he allowed this to happen.

The next day, before my flight left for the funeral, I found myself at a birthday meal for one of my close friends. I had decided to go to his house as planned, rather than just sit at home and grieve. While I was there, my friends asked me about my father, specifically how I had taught him about the Bible recently and how he had professed to believe in Christ. I proceeded to expound the gospel in great depth, as I had done with my father, and across the table from me sat my friend's mother, who was visiting for his birthday. She was not a believer in Christ, and had told her son in no uncertain terms that she never wanted to hear anything about his religion. But she could not be angry with me or stop me, however, because my father had just died! In fact, not only did she not stop me, but she listened with rapt attention because of her sympathy with my predicament. I realized afterward that God had planned for her to hear the truth about Christ, and if my father had lived longer, I never would have had that opportunity. And I knew that if God uses my words to save that dear lady, it will be well worth any sorrow or pain that I experienced.

Learn to be a "spectator" of God's great work in your life and in the world around you. Diligently fulfill your responsibilities in obedience to God, and then sit back and watch as he does all the things you cannot do. Do not think that you can know all of what he is doing or why. As I said, much of his sovereign will is secret, even after it happens. But praise him for what you can see and take joy in it. As the Westminster Shorter Catechism says, the chief end of man is "to glorify God and enjoy him forever." I think a big part of our eternal enjoyment of God in heaven will be learning how he took the clay of history and our personal lives, and molded them according to his perfect plan.[5]

PRAYING FOR WISDOM AND PROVIDENCE

If you want to be the kind of person whom God will lead and guide, then you must be a praying person. Prayer should be as natural to you as breathing, and like breathing it should permeate your life, occurring at all times, places, and situations in which you find yourself. Philippians 4:6–7 says that you should pray whenever you find yourself starting to worry, which is every time you face a difficult decision:

> Be anxious for nothing, but in everything by prayer and supplication with thanksgiving let your requests be made known to God. And the peace of God, which surpasses all comprehension, shall guard your hearts and your minds in Christ Jesus.

Your decisions are very much a part of the spiritual warfare that goes on in your life, as Satan and his demons vie for your allegiance and seek to direct you away from God's will. So after telling us about the armor of God in Ephesians 6, Paul closes this famous passage on spiritual warfare in this way: "With all prayer and petition pray at all times in the Spirit, and with this in view, be on the alert with all perseverance and petition for all the saints, and pray on my behalf" (Eph. 6:18–19).

Those verses say that spiritual warfare is won (and good decisions made) when we have "an everything kind of prayer life." Notice how Paul uses the word "all" four times to emphasize that there should be no time or place in which we do not pray, and there are no excuses for failing to bring our requests before the Lord. James 4:2 says, "You do not have because you do not ask," and that is true in any area of your life, including the area of guidance and direction.

So according to the Scriptures, prayer is a clear prerequisite for making good decisions. But what should we be praying for? We can simply pray for guidance in general, but when we do that we must be careful to have the right understanding of God's leading and not fall into the errors we discussed in earlier chapters. In other words, we should not be praying for direct revelation through some voice, impression, or event. However, the Bible does give us clear teaching and examples of two requests related directly to decision making: we should pray for wisdom and for providence.

Pray for God's wisdom.

As we will learn more about in the next chapter, wisdom is a knowledge of Scripture and the ability to apply that knowledge in your life. And that is what you are asking from God when you pray for wisdom: "Lord, help me to understand your Word better and apply its truth to this decision." James 1:5 says, "If any of you lacks wisdom, let him ask of God, who gives to all men generously and without reproach, and it will be given to him." I am glad the Lord added that statement about not rebuking us when we ask for wisdom. If he never said that, we might think that he would get sick and tired of us constantly coming to him for wisdom, and send us away in anger. But on the contrary, he recognizes our frailty and takes delight in our prayers for wisdom, because they show our dependence on his grace.

King Solomon was given the privilege of asking for anything he wanted from God, and when he asked for wisdom, "it was pleasing in the sight of the Lord that Solomon had asked this thing" (1 Kings 3:10). 1 Kings 3:12 goes on to say that God made Solomon the wisest man who had ever lived. Do you realize, believer in Christ, that you can have the wisdom of Solomon? Through study of the books of wisdom he wrote (Proverbs and Ecclesiastes) and through the indwelling Holy Spirit illumining your heart to all the truth of God in the Old and New Testaments, you have the potential to be as wise as he was. But you must ask God for wisdom, as he did.

Pray for God's providence.

To be the kind of person God will lead, you must be praying that he will control all your decisions and their outcomes. Be constantly asking him to work all things together for your good. But you might say, "Weren't you just saying that he has promised to always do that for us?" That's right. But you still need to pray that he will. A person who does not understand that does not fully understand the nature of prayer. Prayer is not for the purpose of changing God or his plan; rather its purpose is to bring our hearts into line with his will, particularly his revealed will in the Word (and the wisdom that comes from it), but also his sovereign will. In prayer we humbly bow before the Lord, acknowledging his providence and then praising him for how he provides, protects, and perfects us.

I believe that is the primary point of the famous "Lord's Prayer," found in Matthew 6:9–13. In the context preceding that passage, Jesus is explaining how his disciples should pray in contrast to the way pagans pray, thinking that they can persuade their gods to change through "repetition," "many words," or some other method. Jesus says, "Do not be like them; for your Father knows what you need, before you ask Him" (v. 8). The true God is a sovereign God, who cannot be cajoled or manipulated, and who already has planned to meet the needs of his people, before they even come to him in prayer. Nonetheless, Jesus says we should pray, and notice that the things he says we should pray for are things that God has already promised will happen:

"Hallowed be thy name" (God's name is and always will be holy); "thy kingdom come" (his kingdom is coming every day in the hearts of his people, and it will come in finality when Christ returns); "thy will be done" (as we already have discussed, God's sovereign will is always accomplished); "Give us this day our daily bread" (Jesus went on to promise later in the chapter that God would always meet our physical needs).

Jesus goes on to say that we should pray for forgiveness, which God has already granted us in Christ (Eph. 1:7). We should ask that God would not lead us into temptation, something that will never happen, as James 1:13 and 1 Corinthians 10:13 state unequivocally. And finally, our Lord wants us to request deliverance from the evil one, a blessing which we have received and will receive, according to Colossians 1:13, 1 John 2:13, and Revelation 20:10.

As I said above, the purpose of prayer is not to change God or his plan. Instead, our prayer is one of the ways God has chosen to accomplish his plan in the world. And that is the beauty and blessing of prayer. Through prayer we have the privilege of being a part of God's great work, and as we pray, we grow to be more like him. If we do not pray, on the other hand, we will not experience those blessings from God. Divine sovereignty and human responsibility are both true; neither one should be neglected at the expense of the other.

The prophet Samuel understood the connection between divine sovereignty and human responsibility when it comes to prayer. In 1 Samuel 12:22–23 he says,

The Lord will not abandon His people on account
of His great name, because the Lord has been
pleased to make you a people for Himself. Moreover, as for me, far be it from me that I should sin
against the Lord by ceasing to pray for you.

God had already declared that he would never forsake Israel; in fact it was necessary in his plan for the nation to endure until the Messiah could be born from within it. But
even though Samuel knew this, he still prayed for Israel to
endure. Likewise, if you want to be the kind of person God
leads, you need to pray that he will lead you according to
his perfect plan.

So these are the prerequisites for biblical decision making: 1) walking in the Spirit; 2) recognizing God's sovereignty; and 3) praying for wisdom and providence.

If you are not practicing these things, then you have
not been making good decisions (whether you realize it or
not). And you will not make decisions that please the Lord
until you turn from the sins of not obeying him from your
heart, not humbly submitting to his control, and not praying as you should. Before you go any further in this book,
ask God's forgiveness for any such sins, so that by his grace
you can be eligible for his wisdom and guidance. If you truly
repent as David did in Psalm 51, he will create in you a
clean heart, and set your feet on the right path. Then you
simply need to follow him step by step, getting back up
whenever you fall and continuing to pursue his ways.

And the Lord will "direct your paths," or "make your paths straight," as two different translations of Proverbs 3:5–6 say. That famous passage serves as a good summary for this chapter, because it speaks of God's guidance in the words mentioned above, and also contains each of our three prerequisites: "Trust in the Lord with all your heart" [recognize God's sovereignty], and do not lean on your own understanding [pray for wisdom and providence]. In all your ways acknowledge Him [walk in the Spirit], and He will make your paths straight."

DISCUSSION QUESTIONS

1. Paul is an example of a man who was willing to obey whatever God told him to do. Name some other examples from the Bible.

2. What does it mean to make your decisions with "a very strong sense of 'if' "?

3. Practice the "spectator principle" in regard to the events of September 11, 2001. How do you think God brought good out of that tragedy?

4. Give some examples of the kinds of biblical prayers we should pray when we are facing a big decision.

5. Are you the kind of person that God will lead and guide? Or do you need to make some changes before you can receive direction from Him?

THE PRINCIPLES OF
BIBLICAL DECISION MAKING

As we discussed in earlier chapters, words like "feelings," "impressions," and "a still small voice" are often heard from Christians who face important decisions. But as you make both big and small choices, the words that should be on your mind more than any other are Scripture, wisdom, desire, and counsel. These words represent the most important principles for good decision making, according to the Bible. In the next chapter, we will learn how these principles relate to one another, their relative priority, and how you can apply them practically to specific decisions. But for now, we need to consider what they are and why they are so important.

SCRIPTURE

The Bible bears on all decisions you make, in one way or another. Even when you face an issue that it does not directly address, your motives will be involved, and the Bible says a lot about motives (e.g. 1 Cor. 10:31; 2 Cor. 5:9; James 4:3). The other three primary principles, wisdom, desire, and counsel, are taught by Scripture and regulated by Scripture. So it is self-evident that more than any other source, the Bible is our manual for decision making. The God who created human life and the human will has supplied us with an absolutely flawless and sufficient guidebook for our choices. In this utterly unique book he has told us exactly what we need to know—not too much, not too little—so that we can make any decision in a way that honors him and benefits us. As 2 Timothy 3:16–17 says,

> All Scripture is inspired by God and profitable for teaching, for reproof, for correction, for training in righteousness; that the man of God may be adequate, equipped for every good work.

Second Peter 1:3 teaches the same truth when it says, "His divine power has granted to us everything pertaining to life and godliness, through the true knowledge of Him who called us by His own glory and excellence."

Those two verses are pillars for the important biblical doctrine of the sufficiency of Scripture. This doctrine does not mean that the Bible speaks directly to every single issue that human beings face, but it does mean that the Bible tells us everything we *need* to know in order to live a life that pleases God (cf. Psalm 19:7–11; John 17:17). For instance, the Bible does not tell us whether to go to a chiropractor or an M.D. for a back problem (though we can gain wisdom from the Word that may help us in the choice). But the Bible does tell us how we can think and act in a godly way, even if our back problems get worse. We do not *need* to be free from physical discomfort to please the Lord (cf. 2 Cor. 12:7–10), so the details of medical science are not necessary for us to know and therefore are not included in God's sufficient revelation.

Someone might say, "You've mentioned spiritual and physical issues, but what about 'mental,' 'emotional,' and 'psychological' issues? Can the Bible help us with them?" I believe it can, and does. In fact, most of our contemporary "mental," "emotional," and "psychological" issues are so linked with spiritual needs that the Word of God remains the best source of guidance in those areas. Genuine physical problems should be addressed by doctors, of course, as well as by spiritual leaders (see James 5:14–16.) But the Bible describes the state of our minds and emotions as spiritual dynamics that can only be truly altered through the power of the Holy Spirit (Rom. 12:2; Gal. 5:16–25). The idea that there is a third aspect of man beyond the physical and spiritual (e.g. "mental" or "psychological") did not come from the Bible. It is a product of the thinking and teaching of naturalistic, humanistic psychiatrists and psychologists like Sigmund Freud, Carl Jung, Abraham Maslow, etc. And the philosophies and approaches in that secular discipline vary widely from person to person and from time to time.[1]

In contrast, however, notice what Psalm 119 says about the Scriptures. That psalm is the longest chapter in the Bible, with 176 verses, but it is also noteworthy in that every verse in this massive song relates to one single topic: the Word of God. Here are some sample verses that relate to decision making from this great passage:

> Forever, O Lord, Thy word is settled in heaven. (v. 89)

> O how I love Thy law! It is my meditation all the day. Thy commandments make me wiser than my enemies, for they are ever mine. I have more insight than all my teachers, for Thy testimonies are my meditation. I understand more than the aged, because I have observed Thy precepts. (vv. 97–100)

> Thy word is a lamp to my feet, and a light to my path. (v. 105)

> Thy testimonies are wonderful; Therefore my soul observes them. The unfolding of Thy words gives light; it gives understanding to the simple. (vv. 129–130)

The importance of Scripture in our decision making cannot be overstated, nor can the danger we face if we neglect it to any degree in our choices. On the wall in my office hangs a tribute to the Bible, calligraphized and framed, which a friend gave me to remember the prominent role this divine book must play in all my decisions. It is written by an unknown author:

This book contains: The mind of God, the state of man, the way of salvation, the doom of sinners, and the happiness of believers. Its doctrine is holy, its precepts are binding, its histories are true, and its decisions are immutable. Read it to be wise, believe it to be safe, and practice it to be holy. It contains light to direct you, food to support you, and comfort to cheer you. It is the traveler's map, the pilgrim's staff, the pilot's compass, the soldier's sword, and the Christian's charter. Here heaven is opened and the gates of hell disclosed. Christ is its Grand Subject, our good its design, and the glory of God its end. It should fill the memory, rule the heart, and guide the feet. It is a mine of wealth, health to the soul, and a river of pleasure. It is given to you here in this life, will be opened at the Judgment, and is established forever. It involves the highest responsibility, will reward the greatest labor, and condemn all who trifle with its sacred contents.[2]

As Jay Adams writes, "The Bible is called God's law (torah). The word *torah* comes from a figure that means 'to thrust out the finger' in order to point the way. That says it all: Scripture is God's way of guidance."[3]

WISDOM

Other than Scripture, no word or concept is more important in decision making than wisdom. You need wisdom, more than anything else, if you want to make good choices. But what is wisdom? It is a word that is read and spoken often, but little understood. I believe it can best be defined in this way: Wisdom is a knowledge of Scripture and the ability to apply that knowledge in your life.

Wisdom is unquestionably tied to Scripture. In fact, the two words are sometimes used interchangeably in the Bible (cf. Luke 11:49; 1 Cor. 2:7). Every word in Scripture is wisdom, and we gain wisdom primarily by studying the Scriptures (Ps. 119:97–110, 129–130). But wisdom is also an acquired skill through which one can apply the truth of the Scriptures to issues and situations in life, even to those that are not directly addressed in the Bible. Colossians 3:16 implies this slight distinction between the Word and wisdom when it says, "Let the word of Christ richly dwell within you, with all wisdom teaching and admonishing one another." The "word of Christ" is the written revelation we have received from God; the "wisdom" Paul is talking about is the God-given ability to apply the principles of Scripture to human problems.

The story of Solomon illustrates the meaning of wisdom very well. In 1 Kings 3:5–12 we learn how this king of Israel became the wisest man ever:

> In Gibeon the Lord appeared to Solomon in a dream at night; and God said, "Ask what you wish me to give you." Then Solomon said, "Thou hast shown great lovingkindness to Thy servant David

my father, according as he walked before Thee in truth and righteousness and uprightness of heart toward Thee; and Thou hast reserved for him this great lovingkindness, that Thou hast given him a son to sit on his throne, as it is this day. And now, O Lord my God, Thou hast made Thy servant king in place of my father David, yet I am but a little child; I do not know how to go out or come in. And Thy servant is in the midst of Thy people which Thou hast chosen, a great people who cannot be numbered or counted for multitude. So give Thy servant an understanding heart to judge Thy people to discern between good and evil. For who is able to judge this great people of Thine?"

And it was pleasing in the sight of the Lord that Solomon had asked this thing. And God said to him, "Because you have asked this thing and have not asked for yourself long life, nor have asked riches for yourself, nor have you asked for the life of your enemies, but have asked for yourself discernment to understand justice, behold, I have done according to your words. Behold, I have given you a wise and discerning heart, so that there has been no one like you before you, nor shall one like you arise after you."

Notice in that story that Solomon did not ask for more Scriptures. He already had them to study and learn from, and he already knew that the written law of God required him to be a judge and rule with justice over God's people. What he asked for was wisdom, because he needed the ability to apply God's law to the daily needs of the people. God graciously gave him this wisdom, and the dramatic narrative that immediately follows again illustrates the nature of this gift:

> Then two women who were harlots came to the king and stood before him. And the one woman said, "Oh, my lord, this woman and I live in the same house; and I gave birth to a child while she was in the house. And it happened on the third day after I gave birth, that this woman also gave birth to a child, and we were together. There was no stranger with us in the house, only the two of us in the house. And this woman's son died in the night, because she lay on it. So she arose in the middle of the night and took my son from beside me while your maidservant slept, and laid him in her bosom, and laid her dead son in my bosom. And when I rose in the morning to nurse my son, behold, he was dead; but when I looked at him carefully in the morning, behold, he was not my son, whom I had borne."
>
> Then the other woman said, "No! For the living one is my son, and the dead one is your son." But the first woman said, "No! For the dead one is your son, and the living one is my son." Thus they spoke

before the king. [This is courtroom drama, as excit-ing as any movie!]

Then the king said, "The one says, 'This is my son who is living, and your son is the dead one'; and the other says, 'No! For your son is the dead one, and my son is the living one.' " And the king said, "Get me a sword." So they brought a sword before the king. And the king said, "Divide the living child in two, and give half to the one and half to the other."

Then the woman whose child was the living one spoke to the king, for she was deeply stirred over her son and said, "Oh, my lord, give her the living child, and by no means kill him." But the other said, "He shall be neither mine nor yours; divide him!" Then the king answered and said, "Give the first woman the living child, and by no means kill him. She is his mother." When all Israel heard of the judgment which the king had handed down, they feared the king; for they saw that the wisdom of God was in him to administer justice. (1 Kings 3:16-28)

God had told Solomon in his Word that he should practice justice and judge the people fairly, but the Bible did not tell Solomon exactly how to do that in every situa-tion. There was no passage in the law that said, "Here's what you should do if a prostitute comes before you claim-ing that her baby got squashed," let alone two of them with the identical claim! The law of God had revealed much about the nature of men and women, however, and based on that truth, Solomon used his wisdom to fulfill the biblical command for justice in an effective, economical, and clever way. Solomon was so wise that his application of scriptural principles took only a few minutes, saving valuable court time and taxpayers' money. With very little information or deliberation, he cut right to the heart of the matter (and didn't even have to cut the baby in half, to the great relief of the mother!).

As you study and practice God's Word, you can become as wise as Solomon. You have the Old Testament Scriptures he studied (plus more of them), you have his wisdom written down in Proverbs and Ecclesiastes, and you have the revelation of his Creator, Jesus Christ, in the New Testament. As you faithfully read and interpret the Bible, and as you pray in faith for God to give you wisdom (James 1:5–6), then God will be faithful in his promise to supply you with the wisdom you need to make good decisions. And you need this wisdom desperately, because it is the only way to make good decisions on the many matters that the Bible does not speak to directly. But you must seek for wisdom; it will not just "fall into your lap," as it did with Solomon. He knew this, and that is why he appealed to his children, and to all of us, in the book of Proverbs:

> Wisdom shouts in the street, she lifts her voice in the square; at the head of the noisy streets she cries

out; at the entrance of the gates in the city, she ut-
ters her sayings: "How long, O naive ones, will you
love simplicity? And scoffers delight themselves in
scoffing, and fools hate knowledge? Turn to my reproof, behold, I will pour out my spirit on you; I will
make my words known to you. (Prov. 1:20–23)

My son, if you will receive my sayings, and treasure
my commandments within you, make your ear at-
tentive to wisdom, incline your heart to understanding; for if you cry for discernment, lift your
voice for understanding; if you seek her as silver,
and search for her as for hidden treasures; then you
will discern the fear of the Lord, and discover the
knowledge of God. For the Lord gives wisdom; from
His mouth come knowledge and understanding.
(Prov. 2:1–6)

DESIRE

The third principle that we must understand, if we are
to make biblical decisions, is desire. Some Christians may
be surprised to learn this, but God says that your personal
desires play an important role in decision making. They
should never be given authority over Scripture or wisdom, but nonetheless they are significant. God accom-
plishes his sovereign will through our desires, and his
moral will reveals that sometimes he gives us guidance
through our desires. There are also times when we should

make a decision based primarily on them, when everything else is equal.

Psalm 37:4 says, "Delight yourself in the Lord [that reminds us of the prerequisites for good decision making], *and He will give you the desires of your heart.*" It seems quite possible that the psalmist is not saying God will grant the desires of your heart, but that God will implant them into you (when you are following him). But even if it means that God will provide what we want when we are delighted with him, it still indicates that God often leads us through our desires. As John Bunyan wrote, "The desires of God and the desires of the righteous agree; they are of one mind in their desires."[4]

What may be implicit in Psalm 37:4 is made much more explicit in Philippians 2:12–13:

> So then, my beloved, just as you have always obeyed, not as in my presence only, but now much more in my absence, work out your salvation with fear and trembling; for it is God who is at work in you, both to will and to work for His good pleasure.

Notice that God does put good desires in your heart, if you are a believer in Christ, and it is often the best thing to do to follow those desires when faced with a decision. Such was the case with widows in the early church, as 1 Corinthians 7:39 reveals:

A wife is bound as long as her husband lives; but if her husband is dead, she is free to be married to whom she wishes, only in the Lord.

As we will discuss in the next chapter, there were limitations on how far a widow could follow her desires (she was to marry "only in the Lord"), but nonetheless her desires could, and should, play an important role in an important decision in her life. Presumably, she could have married any one of a number of prospects (if she were fortunate enough to have that many) and still be pleasing to the Lord.

One of the recurring themes in the book of Ecclesiastes is that although life "under the sun" is nothing but vanity without God (chapters 1–2, 12:8), God wants us to enjoy its legitimate pleasures when we are living "under the Son" (5:18, 9:7–9). We should also pursue our dreams, knowing that God may choose to make them come true, if they are a part of his will (11:1–6). And since the pleasures we enjoy in life and the dreams we have are expressions of our inward desires, it is not surprising that Solomon presents this advice near the end of the book:

Rejoice, young man, during your childhood, and let your heart be pleasant during the days of young manhood. And *follow the impulses of your heart and the desires of your eyes.* Yet know that God will bring you to judgment for all these things (Eccl. 11:9).[5]

When the "impulses of your heart and the desires of your eyes" are within the bounds of God's law, God wants you to pursue them. In fact, he has created us with the capacity for desires so that he can share with us the joy of seeing our desires fulfilled! That is one of the many facets of being "made in the image of God," because he also takes pleasure in his will being fulfilled (Matt. 11:26; Eph. 1:5, 9). And that is one of the many fortunes of heaven: we will always be doing exactly what we want to do, because our desires will all be fully conformed to the desires of Christ (1 John 3:2; 1 Cor. 15:49; Phil. 3:21). Everything we want to do will be what he wants us to do!

So when the Lord enables us to follow our desires in this life (as long as they are governed by Scripture and wisdom), we experience a little taste of heaven.

COUNSEL

The fourth key principle in biblical decision making is godly counsel. Without it you may wander blindly and regret many of your choices, but with it you can avoid many of the pitfalls and traps laid before you by the enemy of your soul. Consider again the following Proverbs:

> The way of a fool is right in his own eyes, but a wise man is he who listens to counsel. (12:15)

> Through presumption comes nothing but strife, but with those who receive counsel is wisdom. (13:10)

Without consultation, plans are frustrated, but with many counselors they succeed. (15:22)

Listen to counsel and accept discipline, that you may be wise the rest of your days. (19:20)

Prepare plans by consultation, and make war by wise guidance. (20:18)

Oil and perfume make the heart glad, so a man's counsel is sweet to his friend. (27:9)

As we will discuss in the next chapter, counsel from others is important at every step in the process of making good decisions. In fact, we need this counsel to practice the other principles properly. Wise counsel helps us to understand Scripture better, it helps us to grow in wisdom, and it helps us to evaluate our desires more accurately. Perhaps most importantly, godly counsel provides a check and balance against our natural tendency to be biased in our perspectives and blind to our own weaknesses.

At one point in my life, early on in my ministry as a pastor, I was seriously considering a change in vocation. I was talking to a friend in the FBI about applying for a position in the agency's international anti-terrorist division (a less stressful job than being a pastor). But after several months of flopping back and forth in my mind about this decision, my wife Jill called me on the carpet:

"I've realized something recently," she said, "about this job thing."

"What?" I asked, hoping she might somehow settle it for me.

"I've realized that you're being a fool." (Ouch!) And then she explained why: "Because you've been doing this all yourself. It is a major life decision and you haven't even talked to an older, wiser man about it." Then she quoted Proverbs 12:15 (see above), about the fool who does not seek counsel.

"But I don't want to bother anyone with my problems," I protested. "And besides, what could they tell me that I haven't already thought of?"

She squinted at me for a moment, and then said, "Now you're not only being a fool, but you're being selfish and prideful too." (Double ouch!)

Jill may not have won any awards for tactfulness on that day, but she certainly was right, and that was exactly what I needed to hear. My unwillingness to "bother" others was essentially selfish, because I cared more about what they might think of me than I did about making the best decision for the Lord. I was also robbing them of the blessing of serving me. And I was being proud, because I thought I was so smart that I did not need anyone else. But when I finally did take that advice, and honestly discussed my frustrations in ministry with a godly older man, I found that within half an hour my perspective had totally changed. So it did not take much of his time after all! I remained in the ministry, and have enjoyed it ever since.

Some decisions you face may require much more than half an hour of counsel, and for some you may need to talk to many people, rather than just one. On the other hand, it is obviously true that it is not necessary, or even possible, to discuss every single decision you make with someone else. The wisdom you accumulate through studying the Word and learning from the experiences of others will enable you to make many decisions on your own. In those cases, you will be "carrying your counselors with you." But for most of the bigger ones, and most of the newer ones that you are facing for the first time, the amount of wisdom you have will be directly proportional to the amount of godly counsel you receive.

DISCUSSION QUESTIONS

1. Describe the role that Scripture should have in our decision making.

2. How would you define the doctrine of the sufficiency of Scripture?

3. What is wisdom, according to the Bible? How do we get it?

4. What verses in Scripture indicate that God sometimes gives us guidance through our desires?

5. Name some reasons why we make better decisions when we seek counsel from others.

THE PROCESS OF BIBLICAL DECISION MAKING

I learned an important life lesson back when I had my first personal computer. Fascinated by my new "toy," I spent hours and hours playing one of those early adventure games. I directed my pixilated hero around the virtual landscape, exploring new areas and gathering clues in an attempt to achieve all the goals and finish the game. I could never get past one point in the storyline, however, and I desperately wanted to know what happened after that. So I finally gave up trying on my own and called the hint line phone number listed in the manual.

I listened to the clues and then returned to play the game, only to find that it was completely ruined by the "help" I had received! Now that I knew the hints, I played through the rest of the game easily in a matter of minutes, and then it was over forever. I sat there in front of my computer thinking, "I was having so much fun with this game, but now it's useless to me. I wish I would have kept trying without the hints!" The manual that came with the game provided some general instructions that enabled me to find my way through the plot, but withheld just enough information so that I could experience the excitement of participating in what took place. After I called the hint line, all that excitement was gone, because it was then simply a boring, robotic process of plugging in the right answers.

That story provides an illustration that may help us to understand how God leads us, and why he does it the way he does. Our manual for the game of life does not tell us all the details, but merely provides principles that we can follow as we make our decisions. And the Bible outlines a process that we can follow, rather than dictating for us the way we should go at every juncture. We might become frustrated with this at times, because it takes some work, but we need to realize that God is graciously allowing us the excitement of active participation in his plan, rather than ordering us around like unthinking robots on remote control.

The chart on the next page represents a biblical process of implementing the principles we have already discussed. I realize that all the Bible's teaching on decision making cannot be reduced to a simple chart, but this one is merely designed to help you remember the most important issues and their relative importance. It can also be a helpful tool to use when thinking through a big decision. You can pull out a copy or visualize it in your mind, and it will help you to think through the issues in a biblical manner. But keep in mind that although there is an order to this process (re-

MAKING BIBLICAL DECISIONS

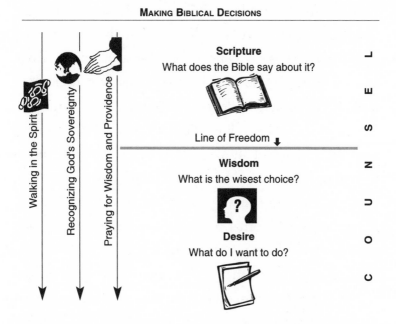

flected in the chart), it is actually more cyclical than linear. In other words, to make good decisions, you will often have to return again and again to the various "steps" of the process. You cannot just "walk through it" one time and be done with it. And you should also remember that the different parts of the chart are interrelated and overlapping, so a change in one will likely affect the others.[1]

SCRIPTURE SAYS

After examining yourself according to the prerequisites listed on the left side of the chart (see chapter 7), the first question you should always ask yourself when faced with a particular decision is: *What does the Bible say about it?* Does

a passage speak directly to this issue, or is there a principle
that applies to it? What does the Word say about my motives
in this matter? Is my conscience clear about it (cf. Rom.
14:22–23)? And so on. This is also the time to consider your
feelings, circumstances, desires, etc. in light of the Scriptures.
Counsel from others is important at this stage, because you
may not be aware of all the ways in which the Bible speaks
to your decision. You also may be misunderstanding or mis-
applying it in some way. So ask others if they know of any
scriptural principles that might apply to your decision, and
ask them to evaluate your thinking about it.

If at any time in the process of making a decision you
realize that Scripture speaks to the issue, and tells you what
to do, then you should obey it immediately. The Word of
God must be given authority in our decisions if we are to
please him, and we can be confident that what he has said
will also be the best thing for us. Jesus said, "Take My yoke
upon you, and learn from Me, for I am gentle and humble
in heart; and you shall find rest for your souls. For My yoke
is easy, and My load is light" (Matt. 11:29–30). And 1 John
5:3 says, "For this is the love of God, that we keep His commandments; and His commandments are not burdensome."

Perhaps you have seen a bumper sticker that says, "God
said it, I believe it, that settles it!" Though the sentiment
behind that is certainly good, it should be edited to say,
"God said it—that settles it!" Whether someone believes
God's Word or not, it is still true and the right way to go.
And even though you might not understand why the Bible

says what it does, or even if your feelings and desires are pointing you the other way, you still must obey God's Word, for his honor and for your own good.

This is why Scripture is "above" Wisdom and Desire on the chart, and in the process of biblical decision making. Sometimes we might think it would be wise to go in a certain direction, but the Bible forbids it. In those cases we must not think we are wiser than God, but we must follow his Word. And we may want something desperately, but if God does not want us to have it (according to the Word), then to go that way would be worshiping ourselves more than him. Such pride and idolatry only ends up in pain, as illustrated by the story of Saul, when he disobeyed God's command to kill all the livestock of the Amalekites. He was following his own "wisdom" and desires, claiming that the people wanted to sacrifice those animals to God. But Samuel rebuked him:

> Has the Lord as much delight in burnt offerings and sacrifices as in obeying the voice of the Lord? Behold, *to obey is better than sacrifice*, and to heed than the fat of rams. For rebellion is as the sin of divination, and insubordination is as iniquity and idolatry. Because you have rejected the word of the Lord, He has also rejected you from being king. (1 Sam. 15:22-23)

"Just do what God says!" is what Samuel said to Saul, and what the Lord says to all of us today. So the most important issue in our decision making, and the first one we must settle is, *What does the Bible say about it?* God's Word is a lamp to our feet and a light to our path, and it will keep us from falling into the pit of bad choices.[2]

CROSSING THE LINE OF FREEDOM

In the process of biblical decision making (and on the chart depicting it), there is a line between Scripture and the other two principles, Wisdom and Desire. This is the Line of Freedom, and it represents the fact that in many decisions we face, there may be two or more choices that are acceptable to the Lord. Many times the Bible does not speak directly, or even indirectly, to the issue at hand, and therefore we would not be sinning against God to go either way. Therefore we have freedom within the will of God, or within the boundaries of God's Word. Neither choice would be disobedient to his commands, so we do not have to fear "missing God's will" in any sense (see chapter 4).

Any good father who wants to train his children, as well as protect them, will relate to them in this way. He will not make every choice for them, nor will he tell them exactly what to do in every situation. Rather he will provide for them general guidelines for their protection, and then teach them principles by which they can learn to make choices within those guidelines.

God is the ultimate Father, and he has always related to his children in this way, from the very beginning. Consider the implications in this apocryphal (and comical) story called "The First Supper," as told by Garry Friesen:

Adam was hungry. He had a long, challenging day naming animals. His afternoon nap had been re-freshing, and his post-siesta introduction to Eve was exhilarating, to say the least. But as the sun began to set on their first day, Adam discovered that he had worked up an appetite.

"I think we should eat," he said to Eve. "Let's call the evening meal 'supper.'"

"Oh, you're so decisive, Adam," replied Eve in admiration. "I like that in a man. I guess all the ex-citement of being created has made me hungry too."

As they discussed how they should proceed, they decided that Adam would gather fruit from the garden, and Eve would prepare it for a meal. Adam set about his task and soon returned with a basket full of ripe fruit. He gave it to Eve, and went to soak his feet in the soothing current of the Pishon River until supper was ready. He had been reviewing the animals' names for about five minutes when he heard his wife's troubled voice.

"Adam, could you help me for a moment?"

"What seems to be the problem, dear?" he replied.

"I'm not sure which of these lovely fruits I should prepare for supper. I certainly want to be obedient to the Lord's will. But I'm just not sure what he wants me to do. Would you go ask him what I should do about supper?"

Adam understood Eve's dilemma. So he left her to go speak to the Lord. Shortly he returned, looking perplexed. "He didn't really answer your question," he announced.

"What do you mean? Didn't he say anything?"

"Oh yes," replied Adam. "But he just repeated what he said earlier today during the garden tour: 'From any tree of the garden you may eat freely; but from the tree of the knowledge of good and evil you shall not eat.' I assure you, Eve, I steered clear of the forbidden tree."

"Well, we still have to make a decision about supper," she observed. "What should I prepare for tonight?"

Adam shrugged. "I've never seen such crisp, juicy apples. I think it would be okay to have them."

Eve agreed, and Adam headed back to his easy-bank.

He was only halfway to the river when he heard Eve's call. He was so hungry that he jogged back to the clearing where she was working. But his anticipation evaporated when he saw her face.

"More problems?" he asked.

"Adam, I just can't decide what I should do with these apples. I could slice them, dice them, mash them, bake them in a pie, a cobbler, fritters, or dumplings. Or we could just polish them and eat them raw. But I don't want to do anything that would be displeasing to the Lord. Would you be a dear and go just one more time to the Lord with my problem?"

Not having any better solution himself, Adam did as Eve requested. When he returned, he said, "I get the same answer as before: 'From any tree of the garden you may eat freely; but from the tree of the knowledge of good and evil you shall not eat.' You know, Eve, the Lord made that statement as though it ought to fully answer my question. I'm sure he could have told me what to eat and how to eat it; but I think He wants us to make those decisions. It was the same way with the animals today. He just left their names up to me."

Eve was incredulous. "Do you mean that I *can't* miss God's will in this decision?"

Adam explained: "The only way you could do that is to pick some fruit from the forbidden tree. But all of these fruits are all right. Why, I suppose we could eat all of them." Adam snapped his fingers and exclaimed, "Say, that's a great idea! Let's have fruit salad for supper."

Eve was hesitant. "What's a salad?"[3]

Your first question, when faced with a decision, should be "What does the Bible say about it?" But sometimes, after studying the Word and seeking counsel regarding it, you may find that the Bible actually does not say anything about it. This should not be surprising, because as the Adam and Eve story illustrates, this has always been God's way of relating to us. He reveals to us some guidelines, but then allows us freedom within those guidelines to choose according to our wisdom and our desire. And the Bible teaches that whatever choice we make, as long as there is nothing unscriptural about it, will be pleasing to God and a part of his plan for our lives. So when we have crossed that line of freedom in a particular decision, we do not have to worry about incurring the discipline of the Lord, nor do we have to worry about somehow "messing up" his plan for us. Knowing this brings comfort, confidence, and cheerfulness to many Christians, as it did to Adam and Eve at the "First Supper."

This principle of freedom in non-scriptural issues is found in various passages. Here are just a few:

> One man has faith that he may eat all things, but he who is weak eats vegetables only. Let not him who eats regard with contempt him who does not eat, and let not him who does not eat judge him who eats, for God has accepted him. Who are you to judge the servant of another? To his own master he stands or falls; and stand he will, for the Lord is able to make him stand. One man regards one day above another, another regards every day alike. Let each

man be fully convinced in his own mind. He who observes the day, observes it for the Lord, and he who eats, does so for the Lord, for he gives thanks to God; and he who eats not, for the Lord he does not eat, and gives thanks to God. (Rom. 14:2–6)

Therefore do not go on passing judgment before the time, but wait until the Lord comes who will both bring to light the things hidden in the darkness and disclose the motives of men's hearts; and then each man's praise will come to him from God. Now these things, brethren, I have figuratively applied to myself and Apollos for your sakes, that in us you might learn *not to exceed what is written*, in order that no one of you might become arrogant in behalf of one against the other. (1 Cor. 4:5–6)

To the pure, all things are pure; but to those who are defiled and unbelieving, nothing is pure, but both their mind and their conscience are defiled. (Titus 1:15)

When Paul says to Titus, "To the pure, all things are pure," he is referring to "all things not forbidden in the law" (and then he adds that even lawful things are impure to the unbelieving, because they do not "give thanks to God"). The same idea is communicated by the statement "All things are lawful to me," which Paul repeats four times in 1 Corinthians 6:12 and 10:23. This principle is often referred to as "Christian liberty," and that is an accurate term when understood as referring to the choices we make within the boundaries of the Word of God (cf. Eccl. 11:9; 1 Cor. 7:39). It is not a freedom to disobey the Lord, but a freedom to choose from an assortment of options that will honor him.

To say that we have freedom where the Scripture does not speak, however, does not mean that those choices are outside of the plan and purpose of our sovereign God. As we learned in chapter 3, every move we make is ordained and governed by his secret will. But here we are discussing our human responsibility and the revealed will of God found in the Scriptures, which does not extend to every detail of life. So from the perspective of our own experiences, we have the privilege of choosing among many options, but in the hidden counsel of God, he already knows which way we will go.[4]

The freedom that we have in many decisions also does not mean that such decisions are unimportant. Even the issues that are not settled by Scripture have serious ramifications for our lives. So how should we decide, if the Bible is silent on the issues? The answer lies in the rest of the process, which applies the principles of Wisdom and Desire.

WISDOM AT WORK

The second question you should ask yourself in the process of decision making is, *What is the wisest choice?* Which way would be the most expedient or profitable spiritually? This question is more important than what you desire to do, because sometimes we desire to do things that are not wise. And though such a choice may not be a sin against God, it can have ramifications later that we may regret.

Paul says in 1 Corinthians 10:23, "All things are lawful, but not all things are profitable. All things are lawful, but not all things edify." In that context he was primarily talking about an issue of obedience—not causing a brother to stumble—but the principle behind his words is the principle of wisdom. You may be able to do something you want to do with a clear conscience, Paul is saying, but think first about how that choice may contribute to or detract from your spiritual life or the spiritual lives of others.

For instance, the issue of where I eat lunch when I am out is usually not one of great moral significance. I could use a coupon and spend two dollars at McDonald's, or I could celebrate California's ethnic diversity and chow down at the Thai food restaurant (my favorite). Either way I will not be breaking any of God's moral standards (assuming that I narrowly avoid the sin of gluttony!). However, depending on what shape our family finances are in, and how often I have done the Thai thing in recent days, there may be an issue of wisdom involved. It may not be best on a particular day to spend the extra money, and if we are really tight, it might not be pleasant to face my wife later, either. In fact, I might be tempted to lie to her about where I ate, and in that case I should do everything I can to avoid the temptation (Matt. 5:29–30; Rom. 13:14). I also might end up too full to eat much of the dinner she has been working hard on, so perhaps I should opt for the quarter pounder . . .

The point is that when we are confronted with even small decisions like that one (let alone the big ones), we need to think carefully about what choice will place us in the best position in the future. Perhaps you noticed that I have used and emphasized the word "think" two times, and that is no accident. In this age of "feel, don't think" and "trust your feelings," the importance of careful reasoning cannot be overstated. God has given us minds, and he wants us to use them!

At this point in the process, it would be good to make a list of pros and cons for the various choices you face. Accumulate as much information as you can get about the issues involved in the time you have, and if you do not have enough time to get enough information, then postpone your decision. All the circumstances that relate to the decision will be crucial to consider, and counsel should be sought again, particularly from those who have been through similar experiences in their own lives. You should be praying for wisdom from God, because it can only come from him (James 1:5), and you should be constantly searching the Scriptures, which are the source of all wisdom. Proverbs 2:6 says, "For the Lord gives wisdom; from His mouth come knowledge and understanding." And remember that prayer and Bible study must be an important part of your lifestyle. The more you ask and learn from day to day, the more wisdom you will have when the need for a decision approaches.

DESIRE TAKES OVER

Many of our decisions, especially the most important ones, are decided by Scripture or wisdom. But sometimes Scripture does not point one way or the other, and neither does wisdom. And when "everything else is equal" in that sense, the deciding question should be, *What do I want to do?* When that question is in its proper place (subordinate to Scripture and wisdom), it is an appropriate one to ask, based on these passages that were mentioned earlier:

> So then, my beloved, just as you have always obeyed, not as in my presence only, but now much more in my absence, work out your salvation with fear and trembling; for *it is God who is at work in you, both to will and to work for His good pleasure.* (Phil. 2:12–13)

> A wife is bound as long as her husband lives; but if her husband is dead, she is free to be married *to whom she wishes,* only in the Lord. (1 Cor. 7:39)

> Rejoice, young man, during your childhood, and let your heart be pleasant during the days of young manhood. And *follow the impulses of your heart and the desires of your eyes.* Yet know that God will bring you to judgment for all these things. (Eccl. 11:9)

Notice the conditions, or limitations, on our freedom in those last two passages: "only in the Lord," and "Yet know that God will bring you to judgment." But also notice that within those limitations, God enjoys it when we are enjoying ourselves. He truly is no "cosmic Killjoy," and that is why I will continue to choose Thai food sometimes when I could be suffering at McDonalds! Thai food is good (at least to my taste), and it therefore is a gift from God for which I am thankful. Remember Romans 14:6 says, "He who eats, does so for the Lord, for he gives thanks to God." That passage was certainly not written with my favorite food in mind—it was referring to meat that had been offered to idols. But its application is broad enough to encompass anything that you might want to do that does not violate the commands of God in any way. As long as it is not unwise to do what you want, you should go for it and thank God that you can!

When we get to this point in the decision-making process, biblical counsel from others is again helpful, to examine our desires and to check to see if we have missed anything along the way.

So that is the process of biblical decision making, or at least the "skeleton" outline you can use to remember its key elements. At this point someone might ask, "What if I do all that and I still can't decide?" Well, that's the time when you should flip a coin (just kidding!). No, my answer to that question would be to go back and start over, with more Scripture and more counsel, especially. This process has never failed me, though I have often failed to implement it correctly, and it has always seemed to help others make decisions as well.

Another question that might arise after reading this chapter is, "Do I have to pull out the chart and trudge through all of that every time I need to make a decision?!" At first you might, if you have never before practiced this process. But keep in mind that we are "creatures of habit" who learn by practice to do things easier and faster as we go. Jay Adams describes this dynamic well:

Think of the first time you sat behind an automobile wheel. What a frightening experience that was. There you sat, thinking, "Here is a wheel (it looked about ten times bigger than it was), and here is a gear shift, here is a complex instrument panel and foot pedals down below. I have to learn how to use and coordinate all of these! And at the same time I must look out for stripes painted down the middle of the road, and signs along the roadway, and pedestrians and automobiles, and . . . How will I ever do it?" Can you remember back to that time? But now— now what do you do? At midnight, on a moonless night, you slide into the car seat as someone else slips into the seat beside you. Deftly you insert the key into the slot without scarring the dashboard, turn on the motor, shift the gears, depress the gas pedal, back out of the driveway into the street and start down the road, all the while arguing some ab-struse point of Calvinism! What an amazing feat that is when you think about it![5]

Good decision making can also become a habit that is "second nature" in your life. As you practice thinking through the process outlined in this chapter (perhaps using the chart to remind you), you will become accustomed to thinking in a biblical manner about your decisions. Before too long, you will be making your choices easier and faster, without overlooking any of the key principles. And then, by God's grace, you will have become a skilled expert in making decisions for his glory!

DISCUSSION QUESTIONS

1. Is God's way of guiding us more like a script or a man-ual? Why?
2. Why is Scripture at the top of the decision-making chart?
3. Explain the "line of freedom" on the chart. How do you know when you have crossed it?
4. When does God want you to do exactly what you want to do?
5. Study the decision-making chart on page 141, then draw your own copy from memory. Use the chart as a guide to think through a decision that you need to make sometime soon.

THE PICTURE OF BIBLICAL DECISION MAKING

Since the Bible is an all-sufficient manual for living (2 Tim. 3:16–17), we should expect to find examples of good decision making within its pages. But you may be surprised to learn how comprehensive one of these examples is, and where it happens to be found. The apostle Paul provided for us a thorough record of one of his choices, and he did so in two passages that we often skim through when we are reading or studying Scripture. The opening and closing greetings in the book of Romans may seem unimportant compared to the rich and profound doctrinal discussions found between them. But within these personal words of Paul to the church at Rome emerges a picture of how this famous and successful Christian made good decisions for the glory of God.

Read the words of these two passages carefully, then use them for reference as we discuss their content:

8First, I thank my God through Jesus Christ for you all, because your faith is being proclaimed throughout the whole world. 9For God, whom I serve in my spirit in the preaching of the gospel of His Son, is my witness as to how unceasingly I make mention of you, 10always in my prayers making request, if perhaps now at last by the will of God I may succeed in coming to you. 11For I long to see you in order that I may impart some spiritual gift to you, that you may be established; 12that is, that I may be encouraged together with you while among you, each of us by the other's faith, both yours and mine. 13And I do not want you to be unaware, brethren, that often I have planned to come to you (and have been prevented thus far) in order that I might obtain some fruit among you also, even as among the rest of the Gentiles. 14I am under obligation both to Greeks and to barbarians, both to the wise and to the foolish. 15Thus, for my part, I am eager to preach the gospel to you also who are in Rome. . . . (Rom. 1:8–15)

18For I will not presume to speak of anything except what Christ has accomplished through me, resulting in the obedience of the Gentiles by word and deed, 19in the power of signs and wonders, in the power of the Spirit; so that from Jerusalem and round about as far as Illyricum I have fully preached the gospel of Christ. 20And thus I aspired to preach the gospel, not where Christ was already named, that I might not build upon another man's foundation; [21]but as it is written,

> "They who had no news of Him shall see,
> And they who have not heard shall understand."

[22]For this reason I have often been hindered from coming to you; [23]but now, with no further place for me in these regions, and since I have had for many years a longing to come to you [24]whenever I go to Spain—for I hope to see you in passing, and to be helped on my way there by you, when I have first enjoyed your company for a while—[25]but now, I am going to Jerusalem serving the saints. [26]For Macedonia and Achaia have been pleased to make a contribution for the poor among the saints in Jerusalem. [27]Yes, they were pleased to do so, and they are indebted to them. For if the Gentiles have shared in their spiritual things, they are indebted to minister to them also in material things. [28]Therefore, when I have finished this, and have put my seal on this fruit of theirs, I will go on by way of you to Spain. [29]And I know that when I come to you, I will come in the fullness of the blessing of Christ. (Rom. 15:18-29)

The particular decision that Paul was facing when he was writing to the church at Rome was whether he should visit there, and when. The gospel had already been preached there (by someone else), and the church that had been established was probably requesting a visit from the apostle. So he explained to them what he was thinking in the process of making this decision. Notice the tremendous confidence he expresses in 15:29 that he and the Romans would enjoy the "fullness of the blessing of Christ." Wouldn't you like to have that kind of confidence as you make important decisions in your life? Well, Paul had it because he made his choices according to the biblical prerequisites, principles, and process that we have been learning. And a close study of those two passages reveals some vivid details that will help you to remember and understand it better.

PAUL AND THE PREREQUISITES

First of all, Paul was clearly *walking in the Spirit* when he approached this decision. He was a believer in Christ who had been regenerated by the Holy Spirit and forgiven of his sins (Rom. 4–8), and he also had committed himself to serving God above all. In Romans 1:9 he says that "God, whom I serve in my spirit" is "my witness"—he was living in the presence of God, seeking to please him with his life. And he was also committed to obeying the specific commands that God had given him: in verse 14 he says that he was "under obligation" to preach the gospel to the Gentiles, because God had told him to do so. Finally, his goals in that ministry were spiritual in nature and not selfish, but focused on serving others. He longed to give the Romans "a spiritual gift" (v. 11), to encourage them (v. 12), to help them bear fruit (v. 13), and to teach them about the gospel (v. 15).

Paul was also *recognizing God's sovereignty,* another prerequisite for good decision making. He made plans (v. 13), but he was not like the people mentioned in James 4:13 who say, "Today or tomorrow, we shall go to such and such a city, and spend a year there and engage in business and make a profit." James says that such people should say, "If the Lord wills, we shall live and also do this or that" (James 4:15). Paul understood this principle, so he told the Romans, "by the will of God I may succeed in coming to you" (1:10). Also notice that in Romans 15:22 Paul says, "I have often been hindered from coming to you." But he never complains about these hindrances that were contrary to his own personal desires. He obviously believed that God knew best, and trusted that he would cause "all things to work together for good" (Rom. 8:28).

To make good decisions, we must also be *praying for wisdom and providence*—and Paul lived out that principle as well. Read Romans 1:8–10 again and notice how he immersed himself in prayer for the spiritual well-being of the Romans, and how he prayed specifically about the choice of whether to visit them (v. 10). In Romans 15:30, he enlisted their help as well: "Now I urge you, brethren, by our Lord Jesus Christ and by the love of the Spirit, to strive together with me in your prayers to God for me." Prayer was an essential part of Paul's life in general, and his decision making in particular. No doubt it was one of the greatest keys to his success as a person, and as a pastor.

Paul enjoyed that success in his choices, and the confidence mentioned in Romans 15:29, because he was the kind of person that can be led by God. Through the power of the Holy Spirit within him, he was able to live out the famous Old Testament passage that he had surely known from his youth:

> Trust in the Lord with all your heart, and do not lean on your own understanding. In all your ways acknowledge Him, and He will make your paths straight. (Prov. 3:5-6)

THE PRINCIPLES AND THE PROCESS

In these two passages in Romans, we see that Scripture, wisdom, and desire all played important roles in Paul's decision-making process. And by looking carefully at the texts, we also get a glimpse of how those principles related to one another in his mind. As an example for us, God reveals how the great apostle "thought through" this particular decision.

When trying to decide whether to visit Rome, the first question on Paul's mind was certainly, *What does the Bible say about it?*[1] That is why he says in Romans 1 that he wanted to serve the Lord (v. 9), use his spiritual gifts (v. 11), encourage others (v. 12), and bear fruit (v. 13). Those were all things God had commanded Christians to do. So Paul knew that wherever he might go, he should be doing these things. But God also had commanded him, through direct revelation, to carry out a specific ministry to a specific type of people. In Romans 1:13–14 he mentions "the Gentiles" and that he is "under obligation both to Greeks and barbarians." In Romans 15:16 he says that God called him "to be a minister of Christ Jesus to the Gentiles." And notice again what he says in verses 19–20:

> From Jerusalem and round about as far as Illyricum
> I have fully preached the gospel of Christ. And thus
> I aspired to preach the gospel, not where Christ was
> already named, that I might not build upon another
> man's foundation.

So for Paul, it was a matter of obedience to the Word of God for him to make plans to preach the gospel in every area that had not yet heard it. (That is why he was planning to go to Spain, by the way.) God had told him to proclaim the gospel where it had not been heard. But God had not told him when to do that in each specific area, what order he should hit them, or even what stops he might make along the way for other purposes. That was left up to his discretion—it crossed "the line of freedom" and thus became a matter of wisdom and desire.

So Paul apparently could have made several different

choices about where to go next, and still have been pleasing God and obedient to his revealed will. Paul could have chosen not to visit Rome, he could have chosen to visit Rome right away, or he could have chosen to do some other things first and then visit Rome. He ended up choosing the last option (transporting an offering to Jerusalem first, and then visiting Rome on the way to Spain). But God had given him freedom to decide, according to wisdom and desire. And those were indeed the principles on which he based his decision, as Romans 1 and 15 indicate.

First, we can see from those passages that Paul definitely was concerned with the question, *What is the wisest thing to do?* Consider the following implications from the texts:

- In 1:13, Paul tells the Romans, "Often I have planned to come to you (and have been prevented thus far)." What prevented him was the fact that the best way to reach all the unreached Gentiles was to start with the areas near Jerusalem and work outward, as in concentric circles (see 15:19). This was simply the wisest way to conduct his evangelistic effort, and he says so in 15:22: "*For this reason I have often been hindered from coming to you.*" There were still places closer than Rome that had yet to hear the gospel.

- In 15:24, we learn that Paul thought it was wise to stop in Rome before he went on to unreached Spain, because he expected that the Roman Christians would support him financially and spiritually. He wrote, "I hope to see you in passing, and to be helped on my way there by you, when I have first enjoyed your company for awhile."

- And in 15:25–28, Paul says that he would be traveling back to Jerusalem first, before heading to Rome and Spain. This was wise because he had collected money from the Gentile churches for the poor in Jerusalem (vv. 26–27). If he visited Rome and Spain first, the needy would not receive the money as soon, and Paul would run the risk of losing it on the dangerous journey west.[2] Also, by building good faith with the Jews, for himself and for the Gentiles, he would be strengthening his ministry and perhaps gaining support for the trip he wanted to make.

So Paul used godly wisdom to conclude that he should go to Jerusalem at that time, and then visit Rome "whenever" he was on his way to Spain (15:24). And the book of Acts adds an interesting footnote to this picture of decision making: Paul apparently knew that he would be endangering his life by going to Jerusalem, but the considerations above were more important to him than his own personal safety. In Acts 20:22–24, he says this to the elders at Ephesus:

And now, behold, bound in spirit, I am on my way to Jerusalem, not knowing what will happen to me there, except that the Holy Spirit solemnly testifies to me in every city, saying that bonds and afflictions await me. But I do not consider my life of any account as dear to myself, in order that I may finish my course, and the ministry which I received from the Lord Jesus, to testify solemnly of the gospel of the grace of God.

It is likely that Paul said those words after writing the book of Romans, so perhaps he was now bound to go to Jerusalem by a promise he had made to deliver the offering (which would be an issue of obedience, not freedom). But either way, that passage tells us that applying Scripture and wisdom was more important to Paul than his own comfort and safety. And he did not let fear keep him from going where God led him. He made the wisest choice and trusted God for the results, and we should follow his example.

Paul did go to Jerusalem, by the way, as the rest of Acts reveals, and was arrested there. But he did eventually end up visiting Rome—as a prisoner. In fact, despite the fact that his persecutors wanted to thwart his plans, he may have ended up making it to Rome much earlier than he would have otherwise. So his desire to visit that city was fulfilled, by the providence of God. And that leads us to our next principle.

When he was making the decision about whether to visit Rome and when, Paul did ask the question, *What do I want to do?* He says in Romans 1:11, "I long to see you," and in 15:23, "I have had for many years a longing to come to you." But notice that wisdom was more important than desire in Paul's decision-making process. He seemed to have the freedom before God to go to Rome at any time and fulfill his desire, but he chose not to on various occasions because of considerations of wisdom (such as preaching to other areas first, and delivering the offering to Jerusalem). So in Paul's thinking, desire did not have authority over Scripture or wisdom, but it was informed by them, and it did play a role in his choices. Perhaps we could say that it would have "tipped the scales" if everything else were equal. For instance, if Paul had taken care of his responsibilities in Jerusalem without getting arrested, and there were no other pressing need for the gospel at that time in any area closer to Jerusalem, he probably would have headed for Rome.

Finally, what about the principle of counsel? The passages in Romans do not contain any clear reference to Paul seeking or receiving advice from others regarding this choice. But he must have had some contact with the elders in Jerusalem, for instance, in order to be aware of the need and situation there. And Acts 21 contains several examples of earnest counsel that Paul received related to this decision:

> And after looking up the disciples, we stayed there seven days; and they kept telling Paul through the Spirit not to set foot in Jerusalem. (v. 4)

> A certain prophet named Agabus came down from Judea. And coming to us, he took Paul's belt and

bound his own feet and hands, and said, "This is what the Holy Spirit says: 'In this way the Jews at Jerusalem will bind the man who owns this belt and deliver him into the hands of the Gentiles.'" And when we had heard this, we as well as the local residents began begging him not to go up to Jerusalem. (vv. 10–12)

A bunch of people were advising Paul not to go to Jerusalem, for what seemed like a good reason. After all, the Holy Spirit himself was saying that Paul would experience "bonds and afflictions" there (Acts 20:23). But Paul rejected this counsel, as Acts 21:13–14 tells us:

Then Paul answered, "What are you doing, weeping and breaking my heart? For I am ready not only to be bound, but even to die at Jerusalem for the name of the Lord Jesus." And since he would not be persuaded, we fell silent, remarking, "The will of the Lord be done!"

The reference by the people to the "will of the Lord" could mean either the sovereign will of God ("if God plans for Paul to be arrested, then so be it"), or the revealed will of God ("Paul must do what is right, even if he gets arrested"). Both are true in this situation. And the profound truth illustrated by it is that Scripture and wisdom must be given authority over factors like circumstances, feelings, counsel, and even claims of special revelation from God. The prophecy may have indeed been from the Holy Spirit—God was still revealing new truth at the time—but it did not cause Paul to jump in a different direction than he was already heading. And the reason for this, I would suggest, is that he had already implemented a biblical process of decision making based on scriptural principles. So the subjective ideas confronting him at the time were subordinate to the objective truth on which he based his decision. In fact, he evaluated this "new revelation" in the light of the truth God had already revealed.[3]

This important principle is echoed by Peter in 2 Peter 1:19, where he implies that Scripture is more reliable than even an amazing, supernatural experience like the Transfiguration (see vv. 16–18):

> And so we have the prophetic word made *more sure*, to which you do well to pay attention as to a lamp shining in a dark place, until the day dawns and the morning star arises in your hearts.

That is why Paul could have so much confidence in the decisions he made (Acts 21:13; Rom. 15:29). They were based on the sure Word of God, on wisdom that comes from it, on desires that are molded by it, and on counsel that is evaluated in light of it. May we thank God for this example that he has inspired in his Word and provided for us to follow.

DISCUSSION QUESTIONS

1. How was Paul the right kind of person, one who could receive the guidance of the Lord in his decisions?
2. How was Paul seeking to follow Scripture in his decision to go to Rome?
3. How did Paul exhibit wisdom in his decision?
4. Think of another example of a good decision from Scripture, and discuss how it illustrates the prerequisites, principles, and process.
5. Can you think of an example from your own life when you followed the biblical plan for decision making?

CONCLUSION

In the second half of this book, on how to make decisions, we have considered the prerequisites, the principles, the process, and a picture of biblical decision making. So it would be fitting, with all those ps, to add one more—the "progress" of biblical decision making. Specifically, *The Pilgrim's Progress!* This famous and timeless book by John Bunyan is a course on good and bad decision making all by itself. It contains so many lessons relating to this topic that someone could write a book called "Decision Making in *The Pilgrim's Progress."*

This book is almost over, so I will not add another one to it. But in conclusion, I would like to share with you just a couple of the lessons we can learn from Bunyan's story. Hopefully, they will remind you of what we have learned in the previous pages, and also encourage you to put it into practice.

The Pilgrim's Progress is the story of a man named Christian, who leaves his home town, the City of Destruction, and embarks on a long and eventful pilgrimage to the Celestial City. The book is, of course, an allegory describing the spiritual journey of everyone who believes in Christ. John Bunyan wrote it while he was imprisoned for his faith, and it is filled with so much comfort, conviction, and wise counsel that it has become the most widely read religious book, other than the Bible, in the English language.

One of my favorite parts is found early in the book, when Christian has just left the City of Destruction, and two men run after him in an attempt to persuade him to return. Their names are Obstinate and Pliable, and at first they both are convinced that Christian is quite mad for leaving the city. But as Obstinate argues rudely with Christian, Pliable becomes impressed with the pilgrim's quiet resolve, and turned off by his companion's blustery manner.

"Don't be so critical," Pliable says to Obstinate. "If what the good Christian says is true, the things he follows after are better than ours. My heart is inclined to go with him."

And so Pliable chooses to accompany Christian on his journey, and as they go, asks Christian to tell him more about the glories and pleasures they will enjoy in the Celestial City. But they were soon to have an appointment with the Slough of Despond (or "Swamp of Despair" in the newer English). "Not paying attention," as Bunyan writes, "both of them fell suddenly into the bog. . . . Here, therefore, they wallowed for awhile, being smeared all over with mud."

Pliable exclaimed, "Ah, Christian, where are you now?"

"To tell the truth," said Christian. "I don't know."

At that, Pliable began to be offended and angrily said to his companion, "Is this the happiness you've been telling me about all this time? If we make such poor progress at the beginning of our travel, what can we expect between here and our journey's end? If I get out alive, you will enter the fine country without me!" And with that he gave a desperate struggle or two and got out of the mire on the side of the swamp that was in the direction of his own house. So away he went, and Christian saw him no more.[1]

Pliable is an example of how many Christians make decisions, even important ones. He was not "thoroughly convinced" that it was right to follow Christian, as Romans 14:5 says we should be about all our choices. He said "*If what the good Christian says is true,*" and "*My heart is inclined* to go with him." His decision was not based on understanding and wisdom, but on his feelings, an inward impression, persuasive counsel, or his desires at the moment. And so later, when the going got tough, he got going—because his present "inclinations" were his highest priority.

This foolish man went from begging Christian to return, then to joining Christian, then to forsaking Christian within the space of a few hours (at the most!). He was like a ping-pong ball, being batted back and forth by his inward impulses and the counsel of others. And so many real-life believers find themselves stumbling this way and that way, because their decision-making process is not grounded in the wisdom of the Word. But the biblical principles we have learned in this book are an antidote to that malady. Ephesians 4:11–12 teaches us that God gave us the Scriptures, delivered by apostles and prophets, spread by evangelists, and explained by pastors and teachers, "for the equipping of the saints for the work of service, to the building up of the body of Christ." And Ephesians 4:14 says, "As a result, we are no longer to be children, tossed here and there by waves."

Another one of my favorite parts of *Pilgrim's Progress* is at the end of the book, when Christiana and her party meet up with a man named Valiant Fortruth near the entrance to the Celestial City. Telling the other pilgrims about the beginning of his long journey, Valiant relates to them how his father and mother had "used all the means imaginable to persuade me to stay at home." "They told me it was a dangerous way," he says. "According to them, the most dangerous way in the world is that which the Pilgrims travel." When asked for the particulars, Valiant recounts more of what his parents had said:

> "They told me about the Swamp of Despondence, where Christian was nearly smothered. They told me there were archers standing ready in Beelzebub's

Castle to shoot those who would knock at the Narrow Gate for entrance. They also told me about the woods and dark mountains, about the Hill of Difficulty, about the lions, and also about three giants, Bloody Man, Maul, and Slay Good. Moreover, they said there was a foul Fiend that haunted the Valley of Humiliation, and that Christian was almost robbed of life by them.

"Besides these," continued Valiant, "they said one must go over the Valley of the Shadow of Death where the Hobgoblins are, where the light is darkness, and where the Path is full of snares, pits, traps, and tricks. They also told me about Giant Despair, of Doubting Castle, and about the ruins the Pilgrims met with there. Furthermore, they said I must go over the Enchanted Ground, which was dangerous, and after all this, that I would find a River over which I would find no bridge, and the River lay between me and the Celestial City . . ."

Valiant goes on for another whole page, listing all the dangers his parents had warned him about! But at the end, Great Heart asks him, "Didn't any of these things discourage you?"

"No," he answered, "they seemed only so many nothings to me."

"And how did that happen?" inquired Great Heart.

"Why, I still believed what Mr. Telltrue had said," responded Valiant, "and that carried me beyond them all."

"Then this was your victory, even your faith," said Mr. Great Heart.

"That it was," agreed Valiant Fortruth. "I believed, and therefore came out, got into the Way, fought everything that set itself against me, and by believing I've come to this place."

What Valiant had been told about by Mr. Telltrue, that which inspired his faith and faithfulness, was the gospel of God's grace in Christ and the hope of eternal life in heaven. He was willing to endure any danger for the sake of Christ, because he knew that he would be enjoying the company of his Lord forever. And if you want to please the Lord in your life, you will find that many times the best decisions are also the hardest. Going God's way will often lead you into risk and trouble, and if you follow the principles in this book, even your process of decision making itself will not be easy. It requires the hard work of self-evaluation, biblical study, and wisdom learned by experience. But what makes it all worthwhile is knowing that your decisions will be pleasing to the one who loved you and died for you.

"To Him be the glory, both now and to the day of eternity" (2 Peter 3:18).

NOTES

Chapter 1: Roads to Nowhere

1 Jay Adams explains the source of such thinking and answers it from Scripture in *The Biblical View of Self-Esteem, Self-Love, Self-Image* (Eugene, Ore.: Harvest House, 1986).

2 Haddon Robinson, *Decision Making by the Book* (Grand Rapids: Discovery House, 1998), 18.

3 Remember that many narrative sections of Scripture describe actions of people (even God's people) that were neither right nor wise, and many times the narrative itself contains no hint that what they did was wrong. A classic example of this from the Old Testament is the polygamy practiced by the patriarchs and King David. This practice is not condemned in the passages describing it because the purpose of such descriptions is merely to record the events, rather than to interpret them. I personally think that the account of the apostles replacing Judas is similar, in that what they were doing was premature, since it was before the coming of the Holy Spirit and the conversion of Paul, who seems to me to be the one God intended to be the twelfth apostle. Even if what they did was right, however, their method would still not carry over to us, because they lived in a time

when God was still guiding by direct revelation and supernatural signs. As the rest of this chapter discusses, today is a different day.

4 Jay Adams, *Back to the Blackboard* (Woodruff, S. C.: Timeless Texts, 1998), 23.

5 John Piper, *Let the Nations Be Glad: The Supremacy of God in Missions* (Grand Rapids: Baker, 1993), 26.

6 C. S. Lewis, *The Voyage of the Dawn Treader* (New York: MacMillan, 1952), 71–72.

7 Ibid., 74–75.

Chapter 2: Special Revelation outside the Bible

1 Charles Swindoll, *The Mystery of God's Will* (Nashville: Word, 1999), 34.

2 For instance, notice how Paul's teaching in Romans chapters 1–4 elucidates the meaning of Jesus' story of the Pharisee and the publican in Luke 18:9–14. In fact, if we never had Paul's teaching on justification by faith and other important doctrines, Jesus' words would be enigmatic at various points.

3 One of the primary reasons many believe that "the perfect" is the eternal state is this statement in verse 12: "For now we see in a mirror dimly, but then face to face." They assume that "face to face" must be a reference to meeting the Lord Jesus personally at his return. But that is reading too much into the text, because Paul is merely using the analogy of a foggy mirror to highlight the difference between seeing something "dimly" and seeing something more clearly. This analogy is appropriate to the difference between periodic verbal prophecies spoken to some in the early church and a written, propositional revelation that can be studied and taught with confidence by all. For a more thorough discussion of this passage, see chapter 5 of Victor Budgen's book *The Charismatics and the Word of God* (Durham: Evangelical Press, 1989).

Even if one takes "the perfect" to refer to the eternal state, the passage still does not say that the revelatory gifts will continue until that time, and therefore it still allows for the cessationist view. Dr. Richard Gaffin explains this perspective: "With this accent on the partial quality of our present knowledge, the particular media of that knowledge are incidental. Prophecy and tongues are no doubt singled out given Paul's pastoral concern, within the wider context (chapters 12–14), with their proper exercise. But the time of their cessation is not a concern he has here. . . . His stress, rather, is on the duration, until Christ returns, of our present, opaque knowledge—by whatever revelatory means that knowledge may come" ("Where Have All the Spiritual Gifts Gone?" *Modern Reformation*, vol. 10, n. 5 [September/October 2001], 24).

4 Gaffin, "Where Have All the Spiritual Gifts Gone?" 21.

5 Gaffin adds these thoughts: "Notice that in the current debate about spiritual gifts many in the charismatic movement . . . agree that apostles—in the sense of those who are 'first' among the gifts given to the church (1 Cor. 12:28; Eph. 4:11), like the twelve and Paul— are not present in the church today. In that respect, at least, whether or not they care to think of themselves as such, the large majority of today's charismatics are in fact 'cessationists.' Anyone, then, who recognizes the temporary nature of the apostolate, needs to think through, in the light of other New Testament teaching, what further implications this basic cessationist position may carry" (ibid., 22).

6 John Calvin, *Commentary on 2 Timothy* (from "The John Calvin Collection" CD by Ages Software). Calvin also adds these thoughts: "But here an objection arises. Seeing that Paul speaks of the Scriptures, which is the name given to the Old Testament, how does he say that it makes a man thoroughly perfect? for, if it be so, what was afterwards added by the apostles may be thought superfluous. I reply, so far as relates to the substance, nothing has been added; for the

writings of the apostles contain nothing else than a simple and natural explanation of the Law and the Prophets, together with a manifestation of the things expressed in them. This eulogium, therefore, is not inappropriately bestowed on the Scriptures by Paul."

7 The aorist tense of the verb translated "was delivered" (*paradotheise*) does not necessarily mean a past action; it can also refer to a current action. So a better translation would be "is delivered" or even "is being delivered." The aorist often takes a "snapshot look" at something that has happened or is happening, and in contrast to the present tense, it implies that the activity may not be ongoing indefinitely.

8 Jay Adams, *The Christian Counselor's Commentary: Hebrews, James, I & II Peter, and Jude* (Stanley, NC.: Timeless Texts, 1996), 339–40.

9 O. Palmer Robertson, *The Final Word* (Edinburgh: Banner of Truth, 1993), 66.

10 Ibid., 134–35.

Chapter 3: Supernatural Signs

1 An example of the disparity between biblical miracles and the claims of modern-day signs and wonders is the sad but true story of a man who put his dead six-week-old baby in a picnic cooler and took her body to Brownsville Assembly of God in Pensacola, Florida, which was supposedly the center of a miraculous revival. The father was hoping the baby would be raised from the dead by one of the wonder-workers in Brownsville, but after a half hour of prayer, the little body remained still (*Christianity Today*, February 8, 1999, 12–13). No such disappointment and confusion accompanied the miracles in the Bible.

Chapter 4: The Will of God

1 Some would add more. Chuck Swindoll, in his book *The Mystery of God's Will* (Nashville: Word, 1999), adds "God's Permissive Will" to

the decretive will as a separate category (pp. 26–28), but it is best to understand God's permission of evil as a part of his decretive will (as Swindoll had already shown in his previous discussion of the decretive will on pages 18–25).

2 I realize that some would challenge this assumption, especially on the basis of 2 Peter 3:9, which uses *boulemai* to say that "God is not willing for any to perish, but for all to come to repentance." They would say that verse is speaking of a desire of God that is not fulfilled. But I disagree, based on the context of the verse, in which Peter is explaining why God delays the Second Coming of Christ (cf. vv. 3–4). If God simply does not want to see anyone else perish, then Jesus should return right now, because every day more people die without the Lord. It makes much more sense to understand Peter as saying that God postpones his return because there are still people that he plans to save (perhaps many who have not even been born yet). This fits with the phrase "toward you," which speaks of the "beloved" (v. 1), and it also fits better with the common meaning of *boulemai*. So the sense of the verse is, "God is being patient toward those he loves, because he has determined that none of them will perish, but that all of them will receive eternal life" (cf. John 6:37–40, 17:1–12).

3 A good "proof text" for this distinction between *boulemai* and *thelo* is Luke 10:22–24. Notice in that text how Jesus uses *boulemai* when speaking of his sovereign determination ("anyone to whom the Son wills to reveal Him"), but then uses the different word *thelo* when speaking of a desire that is unfulfilled ("many prophets and kings wished to see the things which you see, and did not see them").

4 R. C. Sproul, *Can I Know God's Will* (Orlando: Ligonier Ministries, 1999), 33–34.

5 I have an old out-of-print paperback published by Moody Press in 1950 called *The Perfect Will of God*, by G. Christian Weiss. On the back of the book it says,

In fifteen provocative chapters, the reader discovers:

God has a definite plan for every believer.

It is possible to miss that plan.

6 James Petty, *Step by Step: Divine Guidance for Ordinary Christians* (Phillipsburg, N.J.: P&R, 1999). As Petty points out, Garry Friesen's book *Decision Making and the Will of God* (Sisters, Ore.: Multnomah, 1980) contains excellent discussions of all the passages that are used to support this idea of an "individual will of God" (see Friesen, 97–113).

Chapter 5: Feelings and Impressions

1 John MacArthur, *Reckless Faith* (Crossway Books, 1994), 181–82.

2 An example of this inconsistency is Charles Stanley, who I assume would not consider himself a charismatic. But he has published a book entitled *How to Listen to God* (Nashville: Nelson, 1985), in which he teaches that God speaks to us today through the Word of God, the Holy Spirit, other people, and circumstances ("How God Speaks Today," 13–18). In the section about the Holy Spirit, Stanley relates a story about a conversation he had with a property owner who asked him how much he was willing to pay for a piece of land. Stanley writes, "The Spirit of God immediately spoke to me and said, 'Don't answer that.' So I didn't answer. I kept quiet. . . . God's Spirit spoke to me very clearly and distinctly, giving me the proper direction I needed. . . . When I say the Holy Spirit 'speaks,' I do not mean audibly. Rather, he impresses His will in my spirit or mind, and I hear Him in my inner being. Though not audible, the communication is precise nevertheless" (15–16).

It is also interesting to note that Stanley says earlier in the book, "The only time God has used a vision or a dream speaking in my life was after I spent several weeks fasting and seeking to know the mind of the Lord" (11). He then goes on to relate a revelation and vision that he assumes was from God, but never seems to have considered the fact that his physical and psychological state at that time was highly conducive to abnormal sensory experience. I mention that because I have noticed that sleep deprivation and nutritional depletion have often been linked with the "mystical" experiences of Christians (and people of other religions).

3 I added "remembered" because I do think that God, in his providence, brings to our minds biblical truth, and he often does so at key junctures in our choices. So it would be correct to say, for instance, "God told me to share my faith more," even though we might not actually be reading the Bible when that truth comes to mind.

4 Chuck Swindoll, for example, states categorically that "peace is an emotion" (*The Mystery of God's Will* [Nashville: Word, 1999], 49). But I would suggest that none of the fruits of the Spirit (love, joy, peace, patience, etc.) are essentially emotions—though they can *produce* good feelings—because the Scripture says that the fruits can and should be evident, regardless of how we feel. In other words, a believer could be feeling deep grief or serious physical pain, but can still have any or all of the fruits of the Spirit. Joy, for instance, is not in itself a feeling, but it is a genuine gratefulness to God that often is accompanied by good feelings (but not always). Therefore one could feel bad and still have joy, and the same is true of peace, which I would define as a satisfaction that comes from not being in conflict with God or others.

5 Colossians 3:15, another verse sometimes used to support the idea of a personal "peace," is clearly referring to peace between Christians, as the context makes clear (see vv. 12–14).

6 The Bible also never uses the word "peace" in relation to decision making, contrary to our common practice.

7 Haddon Robinson, *Decision Making by the Book* (Grand Rapids: Discovery House, 1998), 26.

8 Garry Friesen, *Decision Making and the Will of God* (Sisters, Ore.: Multnomah, 1980), 247–48.

9 Jack Hayford, "How to Hear the Voice of God," outline from Church on the Way, Van Nuys, Calif., 1.

10 Ibid., 2.

11 Friesen, *Decision Making and the Will of God*, 130–31.

12 This terminology is theologically inaccurate, because the Spirit is immaterial and therefore cannot be "felt." The resurrected Christ made this distinction clear in Luke 24:39: "See My hands and My feet, that it is I Myself; touch Me and see, for a spirit does not have flesh and bones as you see that I have."

13 For example, Chuck Swindoll, in his otherwise good book, *The Mystery of God's Will*, teaches that "God leads us through the inner prompting of the Holy Spirit," and even implies (unintentionally?) that strong impressions are sometimes more important than wise thinking and planning. "When all is said and done," he says about some decisions, "you'll say, 'Honestly, I didn't figure this thing out. It must have been God' " (48). As support for the idea that the Spirit leads through inner promptings, Swindoll quotes Jude 3: ". . . I felt the necessity to write to you." But the Greek verb translated "felt the necessity" (*anagkain*) does not refer to feelings or impressions at all—it is a word that means "it became necessary" or "it was needful" (KJV). And the context of that verse shows why it was necessary for Jude to write the letter (see v. 4). Biblical duty and sound wisdom compelled him to do so, not some cryptic feeling.

14 MacArthur, *Reckless Faith*, 192.

Chapter 6: Circumstances, Counsel, Desires, Prayer

1 Haddon Robinson, *Decision Making by the Book* (Grand Rapids: Discovery House, 1998), 104–105.

2 Garry Friesen, *Decision Making and the Will of God* (Sisters, Ore.: Multnomah, 1980), 213.

3 Paul Helm, *The Providence of God* (Downers Grove, Ill.: InterVarsity, 1994), 130–31.

4 Of course, Jesus prayed when he was on the earth, and now he still intercedes for us in heaven. But that is a practice related to his human nature, as he functions as our representative to the Father.

5 Michael Card, "In Stillness and Simplicity," from the album "Present Reality" (Sparrow Records, 1988). Another example of this misunderstanding can be found in Charles Stanley's book *How to Listen to God* (Nashville: Nelson, 1985). He writes, "If we are to listen to God, we must be quiet and let Him do the talking. Too many of us, when we pray, simply read off a list of requests, get up, and walk off. Instead of listening to God, we only report our requests to Him. How can God speak to us if we don't take time to listen?" (p. 81). Later in the book Stanley says, "Silence and seclusion before God allow Him to speak to our hearts clearly, positively, and unmistakably. Though God may not speak to us audibly, He will move in our spirits and impress our minds. We will know God has spoken to us" (p. 103).

6 Another primer on how not to make decisions is the extremely popular book called *Experiencing God*, by Henry Blackaby and Claude King (Nashville: Broadman & Holman, 1990). Here are some examples of their approach to decision making: ". . . wait till God shows us what He is about to do" (28); "God speaks by the Holy Spirit through the Bible, prayer, circumstances and the church to reveal Himself" (37); "the church sensed . . . felt led" (66); "When God speaks to you in your quiet time immediately write down what He said before you forget" (87); "As I watch the direction the Spirit is leading me to pray, I begin to get a clear indication of what God is saying to me" (89); and "God gives you specific guidance in sensing a call" (142).

Chapter 7: The Prerequisites for Biblical Decision Making

1 If you are not sure whether you know Jesus Christ as your Savior and Lord, I suggest that you start reading the Gospel of John, which is written "that you may believe that Jesus is the Christ, the Son of God; and that believing you may have life in His name" (John 20:31). The book of 1 John would be good, too, because it is written "in order that you may know that you have eternal life" (1 John 5:13). If you want a short explanation of the gospel by a Bible teacher, read *Ultimate Questions* by John Blanchard (Durham: Evangelical Press, 1987). For a longer explanation, read *Basic Christianity* by John Stott (Downers Grove, Ill.: InterVarsity, 1988) or *Mere Christianity* by C. S. Lewis (New York: Macmillan, 1943). And for those who already have had some experience with the evangelical church, I would recommend a controversial but important book that challenges many modern assumptions about faith: *The Gospel according to Jesus*, by John MacArthur (Grand Rapids: Zondervan, 1988).

2 First Peter 2:1–2 teaches this same truth. Verse 2 says we will grow in the Lord by taking in his Word, but the Greek participles in verse 1 indicate that cannot happen until we first put aside our sins.

3 Haddon Robinson, *Decision Making by the Book* (Grand Rapids: Discovery House, 1998), 63.

4 Ibid., 63–64.

5 Some Christians object to the idea that in heaven we will have knowledge and recollection of events on earth. They think that we could not possibly view or remember sins from a perfect heaven. But keep in mind that God himself and the holy angels see the sin on earth, but are not defiled by it. When we are glorified, we will be able to look upon sin with the same perspective God has, never wanting to commit it, but recognizing that its presence in the world, like everything else, will ultimately bring glory to him as he conquers it through his Son.

Chapter 8: The Principles of Biblical Decision Making

1 For critiques of the secular psychological view of man, see the following resources: *Competent to Counsel*, by Jay Adams (Grand Rapids: Zondervan, 1970); *Introduction to Biblical Counseling*, by John MacArthur and Wayne Mack, et al. (Dallas: Word, 1994); and *Totally Sufficient: The Bible and Christian Counseling*, ed. Hindson and Eyrich (Eugene, Ore: Harvest House, 1997).

2 This eulogy to Scripture has been circulated around the world by the Gideon Society in the front of the Bibles they place in hotel rooms, prisons, etc.

3 Jay Adams, *The Christian's Guide to Guidance* (Stanley, NC.: Timeless Texts, 1998), 97.

4 Quoted in Charles Spurgeon, *Treasury of David*, (Peabody, Mass: Hendriksen Publishers), 1:183.

5 For more information on these themes in the book of Ecclesiastes, see Walter Kaiser's commentary *Ecclesiastes: Total Life*, Everyman's Bible Commentary (Chicago: Moody, 1979) or Jay Adams' book *Life under the Son: Counsel from the Book of Ecclesiastes* (Stanley, NC.: Timeless Texts, 1999).

Chapter 9: The Process of Biblical Decision Making

1 The entries on the chart are not meant to be "airtight" categories. For instance, someone thinking critically about this chapter might ask, "But if you are being unwise, isn't that unscriptural and therefore a sin?" Yes, sometimes it is, when we are talking about clear scriptural issues (thus the overlap between Scripture and wisdom). But there do seem to be choices that are not wise, but nonetheless are not sinful in themselves, because they do not violate any clear scriptural principle (such as the example I mention about eating out). So the "Wisdom" section of the process and chart, appearing separate from Scripture, is not intended to mean that you use wis-

dom only on non-scriptural matters. It simply means that sometimes we need wisdom for non-scriptural matters in addition to the wisdom that we need to obey God on scriptural matters.

2 The Bible speaks to far more issues than most people think it does, so be careful not to leave this part of the process too early. That is one of the potential dangers I have observed in my own life, and in the lives of others who have read and appreciated Garry Friesen's book *Decision Making and the Will of God* (Sisters, Ore.: Multnomah, 1980). I think it is a very good book (notice the very long quote in this chapter!), but I also think that Friesen's strong emphasis on wisdom can sometimes inadvertently minimize the importance of Scripture. Readers who come to understand that the Bible does not speak to every issue, for instance, might be too quick to assume that it does not speak to a particular issue, and may miss some principles that apply. In light of this danger, it may have been better for Friesen to call his approach the "Biblical Wisdom View" instead of just the "Wisdom View."

3 Ibid., 165–67.

4 This is another concern some have raised about Friesen's book— that it gives the impression that God's sovereignty does not extend to the smallest details. Such criticisms seem to be misunderstanding Friesen (he states the orthodox view clearly on pp. 201–8), but perhaps he could have been more careful to avoid that impression in some of his wording (for example, he often contrasts the "sovereign will" with the idea of an "individual will," making it seem as if the sovereign will may not be individual, but merely general).

5 Jay Adams, *The Christian Counselor's Manual* (Grand Rapids: Zondervan, 1973), 180–81.

Chapter 10: The Picture of Biblical Decision Making

1 Of course Paul did not have the entire written New Testament at this time, but he was a student of the Old and he received direct

revelation from God, much of which would later be written down in the Bible we have now.

2 The persecution of Christians was going on in Rome at or near the time, and Spain was a border territory known for barbarism.

3 Perhaps Paul's thinking went something like this, "Agabus and other earlier prophecies have said that I will be arrested in Jerusalem. This may seem to contradict the wisdom of going there, but on further inspection it really doesn't. I believe it is right and wise to go there, and on that I should base my decision. Maybe God is leading me there, through scriptural wisdom, so that I will suffer for him. If so, that's okay—better to follow his leading and suffer for him than to run away from his will and end up like Jonah."

Conclusion

1 All the excerpts from *The Pilgrim's Progress* contained here are taken from *The Pilgrim's Progress in Modern English*, revised and updated by L. Edward Hazelbaker (North Brunswick, N. J.: Bridge-Logos Publishers, 1998).

Dave Swavely (M.Div., The Master's Seminary) is the pastor of Faith Presbyterian Church in Sonoma, California. He has edited a number of books, including *Introduction to Biblical Counseling* by John MacArthur and Wayne Mack, and is the co-author of *Life in the Father's House: A Member's Guide to the Local Church*. He and his wife Jill have five children.